A WORD IN
SEASON

An anthology of prose and verse
for use in Christian education
and worship

Compiled by Donald Hilton

NATIONAL CHRISTIAN EDUCATION COUNCIL
Robert Denholm House
Nutfield, Redhill, Surrey, RH1 4HW

Other books by Donald Hilton:
Boy into Man
Girl into Woman
Words to Share
(out of print)
Fresh Voices
Questions Jesus Wouldn't Answer . . . ?
Prayers for the Church Community
(in collaboration with Roy Chapman)

First published 1984
Collection © Donald Hilton 1984

ISBN 0-7197-0410-3
Typeset by Avonset, Midsomer Norton, Bath
Printed and Bound by Dotesios (Printers) Ltd, Bradford-on-Avon

By rhythm we measure life:
Heart-pulse, breath-take,
Summer, winter, day and night,
Spin of the galaxy,
Sway of waters:
By these we live
And keep your time, unknowing.

W. S. Beattie

PREFACE

The rhythm of the natural seasons forms a framework for each year. There may be great variations over the years but the annual pattern is recognisable and reassuring. The seasons also provide vivid images which help to explain and communicate a wider experience. Thus an elderly woman can say:

> I too am in the winter of my years,
> Bearing the glories and the scars of time, *(Item 31)*

whilst a homesick refugee is speaking of more than the natural season when he expresses his longing for his native land with the words:

> soon it will be spring
> once more. *(Item 210)*

The events and experiences of the Christian Year interlock with these natural rhythms. We call on the imagery of Spring to express our convictions about Easter; the New Year becomes a call to commitment. The language and imagery of Christmas would change if it fell in May, and our perception of 'a light to lighten the Gentiles' would have to readjust to a midsummer Epiphany.

This anthology is a collection of material designed to be used in Christian education and worship in churches and schools. The sequence follows the pattern of the year beginning with Advent. Overtly Christian items are indiscriminately mixed with material from other sources. The criterion of selection is subjective; I have chosen those items which I have used, or believe I could use, in my own preparation for worship, and in educational groups.

Inevitably, there is an arbitrariness in the order. Most compilers would have included items about journeying and 'pinnacles of rock stretching into nowhere' in the New Year section, but perhaps not everyone would include items relating to family life in the section headed 'Summer'. Is it because my two sons are grown up, and my own life stands somewhere between midsummer and early autumn? The index will serve as a better guide to the subjects if the section headings seem eccentric to the experience of others.

I am grateful to the NCEC for publishing this my third anthology, and equally grateful to Ann, my wife, since the time I have devoted to gathering this material has often been at her expense.

June 1984   Donald Hilton

CONTENTS

	Page
Preface	
Advent	7
Christmas	12
Winter	26
New Year	37
Lent	51
Easter	73
Spring	82
Pentecost	90
Summer	115
Autumn	132
Acknowledgements and Index of Authors	153
Index of First Lines	155
Subject Index	157

ADVENT

Advent is a time of anticipation. Christmas is on the horizon, Christ on his way. Such specific hopes match a deep human longing that in a world where sadness is always present, 'a day will come, it will come: a day must come'. Even when Christmas is boxed in by secular demands we do not lose the hope 'that there may be a child'.

1   **The reed**

She is a reed,
straight and simple
growing by a lake
in Nazareth.

A reed that is empty
until the breath of God
fills it with infinite music.

And the breath of the spirit of love,
utters the word of God
through an empty reed.

The word of God
is infinite music
in a little reed.

It is the sound of a Virgin's heart
beating in the solitude of adoration.
It is a girl's voice
speaking to an angel,
answering for the whole world.

It is the sound of the heart of Christ,
beating within the Virgin's heart.
It is the pulse of God
timed by the breath of a child.

Caryll Houselander

2   **Peace is good**

When Peace will come, come indeed,
When the dream will finally be true,
When Messiah will come riding on his great white steed,
Solid gold through and through,
And in his hand a banner hold
To show that our expectations have taken place —
Then husband and son, and father old
Need no more danger face
And a little girl will not ask her mother any more,
'But Mommy, who needs war?'
Then in the shops they'll sell
Building blocks and every sort of animal,
While in town and village, little boys
Will no more know of guns for toys,
And person to person will smile instead
For Peace is good: I bet you lots!
No more wounded, no more dead,
No more shelters, no more shots;
And where once there was only the bitter sigh,
You will hear singing with spirits high.

Tami Ha'Elyon, 9 years

3   A tree in the city

At last on the little black tree
In the city square,
There is a green leaf.

Hesitating,
A ray of the sun, comes down.
It is a white finger of light,
Pointing to life.

In the offices,
The row of pale faces are lifted,
They are turned to the green spark,
Unlit candles, wistful for flame.

They are not dreaming,
Merely of distant countryside,
Of passing loveliness.
They know, that loveliness
Runs out, even through privileged hearts,
Like sand through an hour glass.
They want to begin to live,
And to live for ever.

The spark of life
In each of their souls
Is a gem in a locked casket.
It suddenly burns more brightly.
Waxes and wanes,
Like a breathing ember.

Now it could be fanned to a great flame,
By a mere breath.

Will no one come,
Into the city of London,
With the gift in his breath,
To answer,
The people's wordless supplication
For Life?

Caryll Houselander

4   These are the greedy days.
        It used to be
        That Advent was a longing fast,
        A time to feel our need
        In faith and tingling hope
        And keen-eyed looking forward.
        Now we cannot wait
        But day by day and week by week
        We celebrate obsessively
        Clutching at Christmas.
        When at last it comes,
        The day itself,
        Our glass is empty.
        We have held the feast
        Already, and the news is stale
        Before it ever reaches us.
        We cheat ourselves.
        Yet — somehow — still we hope
        In these spoiled days
        That there may be a child.

        W. S. Beattie

5   Come,
        Lord,
        and cover me with the night.
        Spread your grace over us
        as you assured us you would do.

        Your promises are more
        than all the stars in the sky;
        your mercy is deeper than the night.
        Lord,
        it will be cold.
        The night comes with its breath of death.
        Night comes,
        the end comes,
        but Jesus Christ comes also.

Lord,
we wait for him
day and night.
Amen

A young Ghanaian

6   **A day must come**

Drinking drop by drop the pure water,
Savouring one by one the sweet fruits, chewing each grain
    of rice,
For how many thousand years:
Sweat, tears, blood, whitened bones,
Is our heritage now and for ever.

Blades of grass, shadows of tree branches,
Dew drops, foam on the water,
O, how preciously beautiful, White and pure,
Such is our patrimony,
Our People are wretchedly poor
But with all our native country
Although wretched and stumbling
We would rise up heroically.

Our ancestors have displayed without cease
A boundless life force,
Honours and humiliations, ups and downs, many times in
    the past,
For thousands of years one root remains firm,
The tide recedes to let the wave rise and flow forth,
The trees shed their leaves, numberless buds sprout for
    life,
Thus tomorrow, a day will come,
It will come: a day must come.

Ngyuen Thai-Binh
a Vietnamese student who was killed trying to hi-jack a plane to
Hanoi as an anti-war protest

CHRISTMAS

Christmas celebrates the child that 'refused to be different', and in his incarnation reinterprets both the world itself and childhood. Indeed, unless we reduce the season to the worship of 'tinsel on the Christmas tree', the child will grow to be the man who calls us 'to finish the work he began'.

7   The circle of a girl's arms
     have changed the world
     the round and sorrowful world
     to a cradle for God.

     She has laid love in his cradle.
     In every cot,
     Mary has laid her child.

     In each
     comes Christ.
     In each Christ comes
     to birth,
     comes Christ from the Mother's breast,
     as the bird from the sun
     returning,
     returning again to the tree he knows
     and the nest,
     to last year's rifled nest.

     Into our hands
     Mary has given her child,
     heir to the world's tears,
     heir to the world's toil,
     heir to the world's scars,
     heir to the chill dawn
     over the ruin of wars.

     She has laid love in his cradle,
     answering for us all.
     'Be it done unto me.'

     Caryll Houselander

8   The Guest

Yet if his Majesty, our sovereign lord,
Should of his own accord
Friendly himself invite,
And say, 'I'll be your guest tomorrow night',
How should we stir ourselves, call and command
All hands to work! 'Let no man idle stand!

'Set me fine Spanish tables in the hall;
See they be fitted all;
Let there be room to eat
And order taken that there want no meat.
See every sconce and candlestick made bright,
That without tapers they may give a light.

'Look to the presence: are the carpets spread,
The dazie o'er the head,
The cushions in the chairs,
And all the candles lighted on the stairs?
Perfume the chambers, and in any case
Let each man give attendance in his place!'

Thus, if a king were coming, would we do;
And 'twere good reason too;
For 'tis a duteous thing
To show all honour to an earthly king,
And after all our travail and our cost,
So he be pleased, to think no labour lost.

But at the coming of the King of heaven
All's set at six and seven;
We wallow in our sin,
Christ cannot find a chamber in the inn.
We entertain him always like a stranger,
And, as at first, still lodge him in the manger.

Anon

9 A Dissenter's 'Hail Mary'

You bore him, fed him, clothed him, led him;
You carried him, suckled him, sang him to sleep.
You nursed him, enfolded him, encouraged him, scolded
    him;
You suffered him, moved him to laugh (and to weep).
You were the chosen one, you were the maiden,
He was yours before he was ours;
With your flesh the Word was laden,
Seed of eternity, Hope of the years.
For your obedience, your faith and your firmness,
For your humility, tenderness, grace,
Sinners salute you: presume to say 'Thank you',
Who love him and would serve him
    But had not your place.

James Badcock

10 The burning Babe

As I in hoary winter's night stood shivering in the snow,
Surprised I was with sudden heat which made my heart to
    glow;
And lifting up a fearful eye to view what fire was near,
A pretty Babe all burning bright did in the air appear;
Who, scorched with excessive heat, such floods of tears
    did shed,
As though his floods should quench his flames which with
    his tears were fed.
'Alas!' quoth he, 'but newly born in fiery heats I fry,
Yet none approach to warm their hearts or feel my fire
    but I.
My faultless breast the furnace is, the fuel wounding
    thorns;
Love is the fire, and sighs the smoke, the ashes shame and
    scorns;
The fuel justice layeth on, and mercy blows the coals;
The metal in this furnace wrought are men's defiled souls:

For which, as now on fire I am to work them to their
good,
So I will melt into a bath to wash them in my blood.'
With this he vanished out of sight and swiftly shrunk
away,
And straight I called unto mind that it was Christmas-day.

Robert Southwell

11   The shadow of his later cross
Falls over Bethlem's town.
The barren stable is a sign,
His star is in decline!
Yet richness shines in poverty,
True kingship needs no crown,
The Son of Man is dispossessed:
Humility's renown.

Near Calvary's hill King Herod plots;
The child must surely die!
Fierce soldiers search the wintry streets
To see where infants lie.
The holy family flees the night,
Rejection makes a start.
For Mary, thirty years from now,
The sword will pierce her heart.

The shadow of his later cross
Falls over Bethlem's town.
The barren stable is a sign,
His star is in decline!
Yet in the pain of manger-cross
Is life and hope for me,
For Christ brought low in stable bare
Reigns for eternity.

Donald Hilton

12   Oh, hearken, for this is wonder!
      Light looked down, and beheld Darkness.
      'Thither will I go,' said Light.
      Peace looked down, and beheld War.
      'Thither will I go,' said Peace.
      Love looked down, and beheld Hatred.
      'Thither will I go,' said Love.
      So Light came and shone.
      So came Peace and gave Rest.
      So came Love and brought Life.
      And the Word was made flesh and dwelt among us.

      Laurence Houseman

13   **Identity**

      Conceived out of wedlock,
      Born in an outhouse,
      Laid in a makeshift bed
            of unsterile straw.

      Let's trim it up a bit,
      Make the cows gentle,
      Add a sky of soft velvet,
            and bright twinkling stars.

      Let's accent the romance.
      Forget the reality;
      After all it did take place
            a long time ago.

      We know such things happen
      But this must have been different,
      This was the Son of God
            crying and cold.

      Deep down I've a feeling
      He refused to be different,
      That his birth, like his death,
            was as bad as could be.

If it's different
I've made it so,
Heaven, forgive me!
And that's why I'm blind
When I meet him today
    in the addict, the drop-out,
    the homeless, the hungry,
And that's why they often
    don't meet him in me.

G. Betty Hares

14   I've made the mistake of getting old.
      My father did it before me.
    Very soon now my tale will be told.
      The rest of it's going to bore me.

    I've made the mistake of being black.
      My father did that for me.
    Some of them give me a pat on the back.
      Most of them just ignore me.

    I've made the mistake of being poor.
      The world did that one to me.
    Friends pass me by or they shut the door,
      As though they never knew me.

    I said these things in a cynical way
      To a Child who lay before me.
    Most strange! I think I heard him say,
      He has a purpose for me.

Dermot McKay

15   God did not send
into our tormented world
technical aid
Gabriel with a group of experts
he did not send food
not discarded clothes
of angels
even less did he extend
long term loans
rather he came himself
born in a stable
starved in the desert
naked on a cross
and sharing with us
he became our bread
and suffering with us
he became our joy

Anon

16   To Jesus on his birthday   •

For this your Mother sweated in the cold;
For this you bled upon the bitter tree:
A yard of tinsel ribbon bought and sold,
A paper wreath, a day at home for me.
The merry bells ring out: the people kneel:
Up goes the man of God before the crowd;
With voice of honey, and with eyes of steel,
He drones your humble gospel to the proud.
Nobody listens. Less than the wind that blows
Are all your words to us you died to save.
O, Prince of Peace! O, Sharon's dewy rose!
How mute you lie within your vaulted grave.
The stone the angel rolled away with tears
Is back upon your mouth these thousand years.

Edna St Vincent Millay

17   In the light of the Incarnation, childhood can no longer be
regarded as merely a provisional and preparatory episode.
The childhood of Jesus does not allow the Church an
understanding of childhood that measures the child by
what, not yet being an adult, he lacks. Jesus was a child.
This forbids our beginning exclusively with some defi-
nition of what a Christian should be in terms of what a
Christian *adult* should be and then planning only *what* must
be done to turn the child into the man. Our theology of
childhood concentrates on the 'continuous now' of the
child's life, just as we emphasise the 'now' of the adult's
life, without neglecting what the child and the adult will
some day become. A child at any age may be wholly human
and wholly God's. Because Christ was a child, a child can
be a Christian.

Child in the Church

18   **African Christmas**

Here are no signs of festival,
No holly and no mistletoe,
No robin and no crackling fire,
And no soft, feathery fall of snow.

In England one could read the words
Telling how shepherds in the fold
Followed the star and reached the barn
Which kept the Saviour from the cold,

And picture in one's mind the scene —
The tipsy, cheerful foreign troops,
The kindly villagers who stood
About the Child in awkward groups.

But in this blazing Christmas heat
The ox, the ass, the bed of hay,
The shepherds and the Holy Child
Are stilted figures in a play.

Exiles, we see that we, like slaves
To symbol and to memory,
Have worshipped, not the incarnate Christ,
But tinsel on the Christmas tree.

John Press

19   Don't wait for an angel,
              Don't look for a star,
       To tell you the message
              Or guide you from far.
       These are part of the background
              For art-lovers' eyes,
       To help them to measure
              The portrait for size.
                     He's only a baby
                            To grow to a man:
                     To call you to finish
                            The work he began.

       It isn't to Bethlehem
              Shepherds must go,
       But to look for the missing lamb
              Under the snow.
       It isn't on camels
              That real kings ride,
       But on asses and crosses
              With robbers beside.
                     He's only a baby
                            To grow to a man:
                     To call you to finish
                            The work he began.

       Now all you good people
              From bench and from sink,
       Come turn up the volume
              And hear yourselves think:
       Who else on his birthday's
              Put back in a cot?
       Do you reckon Act One
              Is as good as the lot?
                     He's only a baby
                            To grow to a man:
                     To call you to finish
                            The work he began.

       Caryl Micklem

20 Thank God

Thank God . . .
for empty churches
and bursting shops;
for the soldier's Christmas Eve patrol;
for starvation
and gluttony;
for reckless randy playboys;
for tenements
and prisons;
for apartheid-cheapened oranges;
for boring sermons
and trivial TV;
for minds warped by bent schooling;
for drunks
and thugs,
for wreaths made out of holly;
for mucked-up sex
and prudery;
for comfortable affluence;
for ignorance
and selfishness;
for foreigners in foreign lands;
for missiles
and war toys;
for hymns that can't be understood;
for me
and mine.

Thank God for these
else we would soon forget
the world to which Christ came
(and why)
and lose the meaning
in the cosy celebration.

David J. Harding

21   Christmas in prison

From the Christian point of view there is no special
problem about Christmas in a prison cell. For many people
in this building it will probably be a more sincere and
genuine occasion than in places where nothing but the
name is kept. That misery, suffering, poverty, loneliness,
helplessness, and guilt mean something quite different in
the eyes of God from what they mean in the judgement of
man, that God will approach where men turn away, that
Christ was born in a stable because there was no room for
him in the inn — these are things that a prisoner can
understand better than other people; for him they really are
glad tidings, and that faith gives him a part in the
communion of saints, a Christian fellowship breaking the
bounds of time and space and reducing the months of
confinement here to insignificance.

Dietrich Bonhoeffer

22   Did you have a good Christmas?

The waiting is the best of it,
The days the Church calls Advent.
There is the hum of busyness,
The shops are crowded, streets lit bright,
Presents and cards and carols
Fill our common life
Until the Festival itself arrives,
Midwinter's sleep,
And everything shuts down.
The city's daily links disintegrate.
Each family, each unit
Isolate,
Contracted like a sea-anemone,
Essays to keep its private feast
To mark the time,
Or else endure it,
Cheerfully.

W. S. Beattie

23   Well, that's a washout.
God knows where the party was,
But somewhere else.
It figures.
Sit in the car and wonder what to do
(Is there anything to do?)
Near the darkened church where last night
We sang carols,
And also in the morning.
But in the afternoon,
Just for a change,
We went and sang them somewhere else.
Tomorrow
And the next day
And Christmas Day itself
There'll be the chance to sing some more.
You get sick of bloody carols.

What's the use of sitting here,
I might as well go home
And let my mother talk to me again.
God! Five more bloody days.
I suppose carols are better than nothing,
Some kind of way
To be with other people
In an impersonal benevolent togetherness.
Only they will keep on
About rejoicing.
Maybe it's O K for them.
Perhaps they dwell perpetually in felicity.
Perhaps.
Oh come on, start the car,
Get going
Somewhere.
But what's the use,
I take myself
Along with me.

Anon

24   Here is our cross, a sign of the love
in the life of a man
who shows us the way that God loves.

This is the woman
who said 'Yes' to God
and carried the baby
who grew to a man
and showed us the way that God loves.

Here's an old man, who worked with his hands
and hammered the wood,
who cared for the woman
who carried the baby
who grew to a man
who showed us the way that God loves.

This is the busy landlord in Bethlehem town
who lent them a shed with hay for a bed
for the old man, who worked with his hands
and cared for the woman
who carried the baby
who grew to a man
who showed us the way that God loves.

These are the shepherds, out in all weathers,
who heard the good news and came running down
to Bethlehem town
to find in the shed the landlord had lent —
just an old man who worked with his hands
and cared for the woman
who carried her baby
who grew to a man
and showed us the way that God loves.

These are poor people
all sad and afraid
and ill and alone
who saw the Good News
in the life of the man
who showed us the way that God loves.

These are the children
who wanted to play —
more joyful than grown-ups who chased them away —
and found they belonged
very close to the man
who showed us the way that God loves.

You are the people
to share the Good News
of the small children who came to belong
and the poor people who found they were free
and the rough shepherds who glorified God
and all busy people who find a small space —
for the old man who worked with his hands,
and the young woman who said 'Yes' to God,
and that little boy
who grew to a man
and carried a cross
and shows us the way that God loves.

Jan Pickard

25   The way of his coming

Like the gentle dew on a desert rose,
Moistening the petals until fragrance flows
Jesus comes to us as the Spring,
A stream to quench all drought,
The Fount of Living Water.

Like a graceful dove in a prison yard,
Swooping the ground where men walk under guard,
Jesus comes to us as God's Son,
Who breaks the chains of sin,
The mighty Redeemer.

Like a candle flame on a moonless night,
Cheerily defying the blackness around,
Jesus come to us as the Light,
A light to lighten our darkness,
The Light of the World.

Michael Brown

WINTER

Winter has a bad press — and often deserves it. But, like the old age it often symbolises, it offers its own distinctive pleasures. Life goes on through death and winter and the young Mozart can call death, 'this truest and best friend of mankind'.

26   Winter creeps,
Nature sleeps;
Birds are gone,
Flowers are none,
Fields are bare,
Bleak the air,
Leaves are shed:
All seems dead.

God's alive!
Grow and thrive,
Hidden away,
Bloom of May,
Robe of June!
Very soon
Nought but green
Will be seen!

Anon

27 The season of growth

Not Spring,
when tender shoots
are quickly trampled down
and unsuspected frosts destroy;
when bursting life spawns myriads
to keep the few
and thus begets the tragedy of death
within the hope of birth.

Nor Summer months,
when all creation sates itself:
languid, replete and over-satisfied;
long hours when warmth invites unseemly ease
or, sun-denied, breed disappointment.

Not Autumn,
when ripened fruitfulness
reveals the hint of quick decay,
and sombre beauty of the leaves
(so long romanticised in poetry and song)
speaks out for death and death's decay.
The autumn beauty of the trees
invites a requiem and not a feast.

No, Winter is the season of our growth:
creation held in quiet suspense,
pausing for fresh breath
and new endeavour;
when bulbs build up resources for their life
and searching roots reserve their strength,
looking to the rhythm of another year;
when stem and flower fall broken to the ground
and seeming loss is richer gain
as earth receives its food
to rise again next year.

Winter is neither death
nor even slumber.
Winter is the season of our growth.

Donald Hilton

28   The world at winter's dusk
Is hushed and still.
Within the silent wood
Life has withdrawn,
Stem-patterns stand revealed,
Dimly reflected on dark waters
As ice-crystals form,
Lance out, enchant into a frozen dance
The shimmering interplay of elements.
Over black pinnacles of pine and holly
The northern stars are strong,
Akin, ascendant.
Earth now made ready waits
To be transformed into another mode,
Draws to a threshold as, not far away,
The first outriders of the snow reach down.

W. S. Beattie

29   Short days of feeble sunlight,
Biting winds,
Snow, slush and muck,
Icy road surface
And slow-starting car,
Flu, coughs and colds
In over-heated stores,
And miserable queues
For the unheated bus,
The frozen pipe,
The well-timed strike,
TV cut off
And candles running short:
      Our winter!
      You can have it!

W. S. Beattie

30
So it's a bad winter, set in
just when hopes had started — late
autumn flowers. Colour frozen out,
excitement shrivelled at the edges.

Night after night two sparrows
have roosted in the outhouse
yards apart, no flutter response
to my torch beam, their heads withdrawn
into a fragile warmth.

So slight a hold on life, their margin
economy! Every day
they go early after food, returning late.
Down to essentials now, with luck
they will survive.
          We can scarcely believe
we shall survive these grey-long days,
the cold, a seeming absence of love.
Love — is it buried under the snow?
Frozen for ever into the ground?

But no, listen! Even on this coldest day,
day of the worst news, I have seen
beneath the privet hedge the slim shoot
of a daffodil spired straight
as a cathedral into the iron air.

And where the snow has given way
islands of grass show green.
The grass is always green, renewed,
continuing.
          Soon the sparrow
cocky feathered will stir about
singing again and fuss and fight and find a mate.

Love one another. It is not too late.

Michael Marais

31   Winter

Blow coldly bitter over me, oh wind!
And wail your dirges through the soughing pines;
Go bend that gaunt oak with your rugged breath
Till creaking branches crack
And scatter raindrops on the sodden earth.
Be stilled to silence in the bright clear glow
Of frosty sunset, when long shadows creep
And cast their glittering image on the ground.
Then when, at last, the tardy morning breaks,
Come snow and make a sparkling fairyland.

I too am in the winter of my years,
Bearing the glories and the scars of time.
Like that gaunt tree, buffeted by the wind,
My old frame stands.
I will not be afraid, for I shall know
My life will leave its pattern on the earth;
After the tang of frost will come the glow,
A mystic world of deep tranquillity,
And the life sap within me will flow out
To join the Maker of the Universe.

Doris Miller

32   Beautiful old age

It ought to be lovely to be old,
to be full of the peace that comes of experience
and wrinkled ripe fulfilment.

The wrinkled smile of completeness that follows a life
lived undaunted and unsoured with accepted lies.
If people lived without accepting lies
they would ripen like apples, and be scented like pippins
in their old age.

Soothing, old people should be, like apples
when one is tired of love.
Fragrant like yellowing leaves, and dim with the soft
stillness and satisfaction of autumn.

And a girl should say:
It must be wonderful to live and grow old.
Look at my mother, how rich and still she is! —

And a young man should think: By Jove,
my father has faced all weathers, but it's been a life! —

D. H. Lawrence

33   **On growing older**
(A Mother Superior's prayer)

Lord, thou knowest better than I know myself that I am growing older, and will some day be old.

Keep me from getting talkative, and particularly from the fatal habit of thinking I must say something on every subject and on every occasion.

Release me from craving to try to straighten out everybody's affairs.

Keep my mind free from the recital of endless details — give me wings to get to the point.

I ask for grace enough to listen to the tales of others' pains. Help me to endure them with patience.

But seal my lips on my own aches and pains — they are increasing, and my love of rehearsing them becomes sweeter as the years go by.

Teach me the glorious lesson that occasionally it is possible that I may be mistaken.

Keep me reasonably sweet; I do not want to be a saint — some of them are so hard to live with — but a sour old woman is one of the crowning works of the devil.

Make me thoughtful, but not moody; helpful, but not bossy. With my vast store of wisdom it seems a pity not to use it all, but thou knowest, Lord, that I want a few friends at the end.

34   Tears

Glistening, sparkling,
      shining like diamonds,
Like a drop of rain
      fallen from the heavens.
How do they get there? —
      we don't put them there.
They are there all the time
      hidden away
Under a thick, soft pad of wool.
The way they trickle softly, smoothly
Across a land of pinked snow
Is like a sledge of diamond pearls.

Anneliese Appleby, 9 years

35   Lost friends

Never forgotten,
Always there.
An echo of
A memory
Spins round and round.

Christopher Garry, 9 years

36   Lost friends

No happiness, no joy,
No feelings, no fear,
But tears of sadness.

Joy is dead,
Sadness creeps,
Tears flow,
Terrifying cries,
Death dawns;
My friend is lost.
Craters of nothingness,
Happiness, joy, all is gone.

Amanda Bird, 10 years

37 It matters little where we pass the remnants of our days. A few more moons; a few more winters — and not one of the descendants of the mighty host that once moved over this broad land or lived in happy homes, protected by the Great Spirit, will remain to mourn over the graves of a people once more powerful and hopeful than yours. But why would I mourn at the untimely fate of my people? Tribe follows tribe, and nation follows nation, like the waves of the sea. It is the order of nature. The time of decay may be distant, but it surely comes for everyone. No one is exempt from the common destiny. So, we may be brothers (and sisters) after all. We shall see.

Chief Seattle on the occasion of surrendering tribal lands to the United States government in 1854

38 **Freedom**

'Well,' he said conclusively, 'however much you pray it doesn't shorten your stretch. You'll sit it out from beginning to end anyhow.'

'Oh, you mustn't pray for that either,' said Aloysha, horrified. 'Why d'you want freedom? In freedom your last grain of faith will be choked with weeds. You should rejoice that you're in prison. Here you have time to think about your soul. As the Apostle Paul wrote: "Why all these tears? Why are you trying to weaken my resolution? For my part I am ready not merely to be bound but even to die for the name of the Lord Jesus." '

Shukov gazed at the ceiling in silence. Now he didn't know either whether he wanted freedom or not. At first he'd longed for it. Every night he'd counted the days of his stretch — how many had passed, how many were coming. And then he'd grown bored with counting. And then it became clear that men of his like wouldn't ever be allowed to return home, that they'd be exiled. And whether his life would be any better there than here — would could tell?

Freedom meant one thing to him — home.

But they wouldn't let him go home.

Alexander Solzhenitsyn
from 'One day in the life of Ivan Denisovitch'

39   Nice and clinical,
           Don't be cynical.
       No hate,
           Didn't mean to create.
       No love,
           Heaven's above!
       Seemed nice,
           Once or twice.
       What a thrill!
           She's on the pill.
       No she's not,
           What? — eh! — what?
       I'm not rich,
           Silly Bitch.
       She wants the baby,
           Not even maybe.
       I'll not marry,
           She can miscarry.
       Try to forget,
           It's not a person yet.
       Do I regret?
           You bet.
       But it couldn't have lasted.
           Kill the Bastard!

       William Strong

40   The crash

The plane is off its course and flying low,
The night is black and full of flying snow.
The cabin fills with smoke and brittle talk;
Each head wags wisely on its little stalk.

No one suspects the journey is his last:
Some weave a future, some unpick a past.
Some are arranging the affairs of State,
While two arrange a surreptitious date.

Just as the steward sneaks his third cognac,
One wing-tip hits a hill and all goes black.
In the next trice such treasures are destroyed!
Such talents, gifts, accomplishments made void!

A painter's eye, a violinist's ear,
The five diplomas of the engineer,
The ten languages of the refugee,
An Oxford accent from the BBC,

An actor's profile, like a Grecian god's,
The laird's dexterity with fishing-rods,
The bishop's knowledge of the Coptic Church —
All is annihilated in one lurch.

Nothing's now gained by being six-foot four.
Nothing can possibly matter any more
Of stature, or of birth or fame or mind,
But whether one was humble and was kind.

Dermot McKay

41   Since death (properly understood) is the true, ultimate
      purpose of life, I have for several years past made myself
      acquainted with this truest and best friend of mankind so
      that he has for me, not only nothing terrifying any more,
      but much that is tranquilising and consoling. And I thank
      God that he has bestowed on me the good fortune of
      providing the opportunity (you understand me) of
      recognising death as the key to our true blessedness. I never
      lie down in my bed without reflecting that perhaps I (young
      as I am) shall never see another day; yet none of all who
      know me can say that I am socially melancholy or morose.
      For this blessing I daily thank my Creator and wish it from
      my heart for all my fellow man.

      W. A. Mozart in a letter to his dying father

42   If I should go before the rest of you
Break not a flower nor inscribe a stone,
Nor when I'm gone speak in a Sunday voice
But be the usual selves that I have known.

Weep if you must,
Parting is hell,
But life goes on,
So sing as well.

Joyce Grenfell

43   If you leave me I shall not die,
Nor make grief a trumpet to shatter the sky.
I shall not ask for anything more
Than to walk according to natural law,
One foot behind, the other before.
I shall wake at morning
And sleep at night,
And tell, unfailing,
Black from white.
I shall use my brains
To earn my bread,
Snarl when hungry,
Smile well fed.
I shall not die;
I shall be dead.

Anon

44   Death is nothing at all, I have only slipped away into the next room. I am I and you are you. Whatever we were to each other that we are still. Call me by my old familiar name, speak to me in the easy way you always used. Put no difference into your tone, wear no forced air of solemnity or sorrow . . . What is this death but a negligible accident? Why should I be out of mind because I am out of sight? I am waiting for you, for an interval, somewhere very near just around the corner. ALL IS WELL.

Anon

NEW YEAR

The first minute of the new year is no different in itself than the dying moment of the year just gone, but it feels different. New hopes dawn. We are pilgrims again and find the 'faith to live by what we cannot prove'. Set near the beginning of the year, the Week of Prayer for Christian Unity speaks not only of the Church but of the unity of creation and human life upon which our very living depends.

45   I believe that nothing in life is unimportant — that every moment can be a beginning, and is a time for decision taken against the constant background of one's faith.

     Each word and gesture, whether it comes from strength or weakness, may change the subsequent course of our life, or the life of those around us.

Roger Bannister

46   **Mist**

Starting on the hill we walk in sun
and see the blinding mist below —
concealing what? We do not know.
Then, as the path leads down
from height and light,
the mist appears to part;
it clears around us.
But, looking back, we cannot see
the hill we thought we knew,
for it is thickly hid in cloud.

And so, for us, the world's a shining disc
that follows as we wander through the mist.

A. F. West

47   You
       In this New Year
       What do you hope for?

       Then there was a silence.

       Hope for?
       Hope that, many things:
       That life continues tolerable,
       That this is not the year
       Of the unknown calamity,
       That I will cope,
       That this, that that.

       Then several things we named
       Within the world
       That we could hope
       At a safe distance.

       Hope for? Yourself? That's different.
       Hope for is let into the heart
       To dare a real possibility
       To risk a loss.
       Hope for is dangerous.

       And to display it publicly,
       To pin it down, and categorise,
       And say, this is my hope and that is not,
       Congeal into a frozen sentiment,
       A proposition for debate,
       What should be flowing, open-ended, free . . .

       It's not like that.
       Somewhere within, I hope;
       But hardly dare admit it to myself,
       Or know for what,
       Lest it grow huge, self-fed,
       And overwhelm the actual,
       The present moment
       To make it savourless.

I do not live by hoping
But in the things that fall to me to do
Today, this week, perhaps the next.
No further. If within your mind
You live ahead much more
The weight becomes too heavy,
Uncontrollable.

Yet somewhere, like a thread
Through duty, through the interlocked routines
With which I juggle daily,
Is a light of hope,
Elusive and enduring.

W. S. Beattie

48   Time

Time to me is the plants that grow in rain,
And the sea creeping up the sand,
Time to me is the clouds which sail the skies,
And fish that glide through the sea,
The moss that grows upon the wall,
It all takes time.

Michael Boore, 10 years

49   The mountains of the moon

The towering peaks and pinnacles of rock stretching into
    nowhere.
A landscape of darkness and dereliction.
An imaginary darkness lapping at my feet.
The travelling hillside of space,
Travelling up, up and up,
Up into nowhere.
The Hills towering over peaks,
The peaks are colonies of darkness.

Ian Rollison, 9 years

50   Life-long, *or* Horizon of life

My gaze travels down the cliff onto the shingle,
Travels across the rocks
Onto the sand,
Into the sea.
Feathery breakers dancing, singing,
Below becalmed heavens.

And I think before me,
Into what, Life alone knows.

Into the dawn
When the sun shall bring back to life
The sleeping radiance of the night.
A lonesome gull shatters my mind
Its mournful cry piercing the silence
But only vaguely.

I know of nothing but happiness,
The vast space behind me;
The prairie is my life,
The few trees and shrubs, happenings.
Rabbit warrens homes that my life has rested in,
And myself, centre of these thoughts,
Resting under an ever-lowering sun
The ever-deepening red and gold sky
In the heart of nature.
The buttercups waver around me.
A ghost of mist touches me with fingers
That dissolve into my hair.

I carelessly chew grass stalk
And sniff the cool air of the evening.
The gilded waves lap, subdued, against the shore.

No words shall ever describe
How I feel now.
On this evening,
Where I sit.
And a secret wraps round my brain
That none shall ever know.

The secret of peace.

Kate Rambridge, 8 years

51 'I am the Way'

Thou art the Way.
Hadst thou been nothing but the goal,
　I cannot say
If thou hadst ever met my soul.

　I cannot see —
I, child of process — if there lies
　An end for me,
Full of repose, full of replies.

　I'll not reproach
The road that winds, my feet that err.
　Access, approach
Art thou, Time, Way, and Wayfarer.

Alice Meynell

52 Sunday and every day

Travelling
Along the ridge, along the valley
Over the river, over the plain
East, West, South, North —
Paths as varied as there are people
Wayfaring

Travelling
With straight flight homing in
Or wandering through half the county,
In jostling crowds, in busy traffic
Or solitary on the road
Until its ending

Travelling
Along the way
Towards our rendezvous,
To a half-way house we call 'a church'
To a staging point that we call 'death'
To a destination we call 'God'

Travelling

W. S. Beattie

53 To Colonel Alexei Leonov
(The first man to walk in space)

So you stepped out of your space capsule
Into nothing
Where man had never been before
You hovered in a partial vacuum
Hazarding all upon a theory.
No one had done before what you have done
No one could be quite sure what you would meet.
Of course they made their calculations,
Caution had carefully prepared for what might be,
But no one could be sure.
Until you clambered out
Man's dream remained
A wistful longing, unfulfilled.
But you made out of it
Reality.

And so you gave man freedom to explore
A medium beyond
The envelope of atmosphere, his home.
New worlds are his
Not only hemispheres,
Infinite of space
With only time to check his wanderings.
And all this came
From opening a door
And stepping into
The Unknown.

Lord, make us men *people* of faith:
Faith to trust in what we hope for,
Faith to live by what we cannot prove
Until we risk ourselves upon it
With our lives.
Teach us by man's *humanity's* conquest of the world,
By those who ventured on a dream
And found new continents, new truth, new power
By faith.
Teach us to trust the hopes we have been given
The hope of peace and welfare for mankind,
The hope that love means more than hate,
The hope that death is not the cynical denial
Of all that man *humanity* has hoped for.

Teach us to take these and to live by them
And so to find that liberty from fear,
And live as free men in a world
Where man is called to live by faith
Or to withdraw
A frightened beast, defeated by reality.

Teach us to live
As Jesus lived
Who took the hopes of men
And made them real
By stepping out of safe convention
Into love.
And so he gave us freedom
 By his faith.

Jim Bates

54   Faith

How do I know that God is good? I don't.
I gamble like a man. I bet my life
Upon one side in life's great war. I must,
I can't stand out. I must take sides. The man
Who is a neutral in this fight is not
A man. He's bulk and body without breath,
Cold leg of lamb without mint sauce. A fool.
He makes me sick. Good Lord! Weak tea! Cold slops!
I want to live, live out, not wobble through
My life somehow, and then into the dark.
I must have God . . .
                    . . . How is it proved?
It isn't proved, you fool, it can't be proved.
How can you prove a victory before
It's won? How can you prove a man who leads,
To be a leader worth the following,
Unless you follow to the death — and out
Beyond mere death, which is not anything
But Satan's lie upon eternal life?
Well — God's my leader, and I hold that he
Is good, and strong enough to work his plan
And purpose out to its appointed end.

G. A. Studdert Kennedy

55   The Week of Prayer for Christian Unity

We seek the unity
Within diversity.
Christ blesses our meeting
And each loving greeting.
God can make all things new.

Kinship of mind and heart
Forbids us ever part.
Service and worship, both
Dismiss our ancient wrath,
For God makes all things new.

Together, let us pray
And praying, therefore, stay
Travellers along the way
Until the glorious day
When God makes all things new.

Donald Hilton

56   In Omnibus Unitas

We are all one, whatever we may say.
The warp minded beggar, wending her weak way
Across the garden, is a part of me
And will be throughout all eternity.
Whate'er I do or say is part of them
And must concern all these, my fellowmen.
We cannot live unto ourselves alone
If God upon the throne of our frail hearts is reigning;
For if we love him and he made all,
Then we are one, and follow, at his call
To live out here, on earth, our puny lives
According to his way. And whosoever strives
With peace t'wards all men, just to do his will,
Will find him in them, e'en through good or ill,
He the true end of all our feeble striving.

Sister Mary Anselm

57   To an earthworm

You worm!
Despised of man,
Trodden underfoot,
Cast to the hungry robin, tempting him to stay,
Or yet ignored, as spade bites deeper into frosty earth.

And yet . . .
Beneath the moving earth
Where noisy revolution
Is silent
To deaf man
You work your works with patience
And with zeal.

Piercing, you cast the earth behind you,
Miniature torrents follow in your stead,
Life-giving
And renewing.
Soil breaks on soil and earth begins to breathe,
Whilst all the myriad creatures aid your part;
Releasing life
And hope for eager roots.

You worm!
Despised of man in ignorant conceit.
But coveted by earth, feeding on your labours
And offering its unity to Him.

Donald Hilton

58   The world is passing through troubled times. The young people of today think of nothing but themselves. They have no reverence for parents or old age; they are impatient of all restraint; they talk as if they alone knew everything, and what passes for wisdom with us is foolishness with them. As for the girls, they are foolish and immodest and unwomanly in speech, behaviour and dress.

Peter the Hermit, 1274

59   I have not had leisure to give the public an earlier account of my plan for a reform of the rising generation by establishing schools where poor children may be received upon the Sunday and there engaged in learning to read and to repeat their catechism or anything else that may be deemed proper to open their minds to a knowledge of their duty to God, to their neighbours, and themselves. The utility of an establishment of this sort was first suggested by a group of miserable little wretches whom I observed one day in the street where many people employed in the pin manufactory reside. I was expressing my concern to one at their forlorn and neglected state, and was told that if I were to pass through that street upon Sundays it would shock me indeed to see the crowds of children who were spending that sacred day in noise and riot, to the extreme annoyance of all decent people. I immediately determined to make some little effort to remedy the evil. Having found four persons who had been accustomed to instruct children in reading, I engaged to pay the sum they required for receiving and instructing such children as I should send to them every Sunday. The children were to come soon after ten in the morning and stay till twelve; they were then to go home and return at one, and after reading a lesson they were to be conducted to church. After church they were to be employed in repeating the catechism till half past five, and then to be dismissed, with an injunction to go home without making a noise, and by no means to play in the streets. This was the general outline of the regulations.

Robert Raikes

60   A day is like a journey,
We pass from morn to night.

School is like a journey,
From class one to the top.

A year is like a journey,
Through seasons, months and weeks.

Life is like a journey,
And we are stepping out.

Father God, in all our journeys
Be with us.

Donald Hilton

61   **What's in earth?**

While you're walking along, do you ever wonder
What's beneath you, deep down under?

Down below there's a lot going on
Under the path that we're walking along:
Little roots, big roots, tunnelling moles,
Rabbits in burrows and worms in their holes.

While you're walking along, do you ever wonder
What's beneath you, deep down under?

Is there coal down there where the miners toil?
Or salt perhaps. Or clay. Or oil.
Have you ever thought what the earth is giving
To make us happy and keep us living?

Anita Hewett

62   The earth

Listen, I am the earth
I cover the whole world over,
Above me is air and ocean
River and lake,
I spread beneath your feet,
You walk on me.
Tread softly.
Seeds planted in me grow
Nourished by the richness of my soil
Their roots burrowing down
Holding firmly to me
As they sway in the breeze
Or the waters flow.
Plants in the air,
Weeds in the water,
I make everything grow.

Anon

63   And he showed me more, a little thing, the size of a hazelnut, on the palm of my hand, round like a ball. I looked at
it thoughtfully and wondered, 'What is this?' And the
answer came, 'It is all that is made.' I marvelled that it
continued to exist and did not suddenly disintegrate; it was
so small. And again my mind supplied the answer, 'It
exists, both now and for ever, because God loves it.'

Lady Julian of Norwich

64   I and my rose

There is a world of wonder in this rose;
God made it, and his whole creation grows
To a point of perfect beauty
In this garden plot. He knows
The poet's thrill
On this June morning, as he sees
His will
To beauty taking form, his word
Made flesh, and dwelling among men.
All mysteries
In this one flower meet
And intertwine,
The universal is concrete
The human and divine,
In one unique and perfect thing, are fused
Into a unit of Love,
This rose as I behold it;
For all things gave it me,
The stars have helped to mould it,
The air, soft moonshine, and the rain,
The meekness of old mother earth,
The many-billowed sea.
The evolution of ten million years,
And all the pain
Of ages, brought it to its birth
And gave it me.
The tears
Of Christ are in it,
And his blood
Has dyed it red,
I could not see it but for him
Because he led
Me to the love of God,
From which all Beauty springs.
I and my rose
Are one.

G. A. Studdert Kennedy

65   Ways of learning

'Today I will teach you roses.
Look!' I looked
And saw a bush, in subtle balance,
Pleasure to the eye,
With golden flowers, swaying in the breeze.
Then I looked closer, saw how it was made,
Each single part built up, to the last molecule.
So. This is a rose.

'Now close your eyes
And let me lead you.
Here. Inhale. What do you smell?'
The scent was sweet, intoxicating,
Wayward, elusive in the wind.
This too is a rose?

So sweet the scent, how must it taste?
'Bend down and eat, if you desire.'
I bent, and ate, and found it hard.
It was a bitter swallowing,
My mouth was torn and bleeding.
And is this a rose?

'Since you are pain-struck and perplexed
Turn once again. Now sit,
Be very still and listen.'
So I did
As I was bid,
And heard the wind among the leaves.
No more.
The life of cell and bud and root
To me was silence, imperceptible.
I don't know how to listen to a rose.

'There's only one thing left to do,
So touch it,
Hold it gently in your hands,
Let it touch you.'
I can't tell what a rose is
In itself.
But, if it will,
I may submit to let it teach me
As the wind blows
Still.

W. S. Beattie

LENT

Made in his image we seek to compress God into ours. The Christ who comes anonymously so that we may discover him for ourselves can both comfort and disturb us. Our descriptions of him never quite match our experience of this Lord who is 'our true mother, Jesus', a 'disturber of religious comfort' and 'a friend of wine imbibers and harlots'. In the total pattern of growth our discipleship varies. Mary needs Martha and even Judas plays his part.

66   Is this a Fast, to keep
                    The Larder leane?
                    And cleane
        From fat of Veales and sheep?

        Is it to quit the dish
                    Of Flesh, yet still
                    To fill
        The platter high with Fish?

        Is it to faste an houre,
                    Or rag'd to go,
                    Or show
        A downcast look, and sowre?

        No: 'tis a Fast, to dole
                    Thy sheaf of wheat
                    And meat
        Unto the hungry soule.

        It is to fast from strife,
                    From old debate,
                    And hate;
        To circumcise thy life.

        To shew a heart grief-rent;
                    To starve thy sin,
                    Not Bin;
        And that's to keep thy Lent.

        Robert Herrick

67   The hand

First, it comes as a baby's hand, so soft and appealing, that
the hardest heart must melt at its touch;
Then, as a hand rough and hard with toil, so that the
poorest of us need not be ashamed to put our hand into it;
And last, as a hand all pierced and wounded, so that we
may know that there is no sorrow that can come to us which
has not already been felt and borne by thee and borne
gladly.

Anon

68   I met a stranger yestere'en:
I put food in the eating place,
Drink in the drinking place,
Music in the listening place.
And in the sacred name of the Triune,
He blessed myself and my house,
My cattle and my dear ones;
And the lark sang in his song,
     often, often, often
Comes the Christ in stranger's guise
     often, often, often
Comes the Christ in stranger's guise.

Ancient Celtic rune

69   He comes to us as one unknown, without a name, as of old,
by the lake-side, he came to those men who knew him not.
He speaks to us the same word: 'Follow thou me!' and sets
us to the tasks which he has to fulfil for our time. He
commands. And to those who obey him, whether they be
wise or simple, he will reveal himself in the toils, the
conflicts, the sufferings which they shall pass through in
his fellowship, and as an ineffable mystery, they shall learn
in their own experience who he is.

Albert Schweitzer

70 What is meant when we say that we must be 'like Jesus'? It may be that most people tend to find in Jesus (if they look at him at all) a vindication of a life-style which they have already chosen for themselves for other reasons. If you are a priest you see in Jesus the epitome of the great High Priest. If you are a layman Jesus does not look like a priest at all. He is seen as the most lay of all great spiritual leaders. If you are a radical, you take your inspiration from the Jesus who came to turn the world upside down. If you are a conservative, you rejoice that Jesus said that not one jot or tittle of tradition would be altered. If you are a quiet man, you see in Jesus the one who was always withdrawing into a desert place for peace and meditation. If you are a man of action, Jesus is seen as the dynamic leader who was always to be found in the thick of every conflict. If you are a pacifist, Jesus is on your side because he urged his followers to turn the other cheek. If you are a militarist, you are glad he drove the corrupt traders from the temple with a scourge of cords. If you are a lover of good things, Jesus is your man. He was often criticised because he was a friend of wine imbibers and harlots. If you are a Puritan at heart, you are glad to follow the one who set so little store by worldly pleasures that he had nowhere to lay his head.

Is it a matter of paying your money and taking your choice? Or is it really because Jesus was a man for all seasons?

Edward Patey

71   There are people after Jesus.
      They have seen the signs.
      Quick, let's hide him.
      Let's think; carpenter,
                  fisherman's friend,
                  disturber of religious comfort.
      Let's award him a degree in theology,
      a purple cassock
      and a position of respect.
      They'll never think of looking here.
      Let's think;
      his dialect may betray him,
      his tongue is of the masses.
      Let's teach him Latin
      and seventeenth century English,
      they'll never think of listening in.
      Let's think;
      humble,
      Man of Sorrows,
      nowhere to lay his head.
      We'll build a house for him,
      somewhere away from the poor.
      We'll fill it with brass and silence.
      It's sure to throw them off.

      There are people after Jesus.
      Quick, let's hide him.

      Steve Turner

72   What happened to me as the work (of translating the New
      Testament) progressed was that the figure of Jesus
      emerged more and more clearly, and in a way
      unexpectedly. Of course I had a deep respect, indeed a
      great reverence, for the conventional Jesus Christ whom
      the Church worshipped. But I was not at all prepared for
      the unconventional man revealed in these terse Gospels.
      No one could possibly have invented such a person: this
      was no puppet-hero built out of the imaginations of adoring
      admirers. 'This man Jesus' so briefly described, rang true,
      sometimes alarmingly true. I began to see now why the

religious Establishment of those days wanted to get rid of him at all costs. He was sudden death to pride, pomposity and pretence . . .

The record of the behaviour of Jesus on the way to the cross and of the crucifixion itself is almost unbearable, chiefly because it is so intensely human. If, as I believe, this was indeed God focused in a human being, we can see for ourselves that here is no play-acting, this is the real thing. There are no supernatural advantages for this man. No celestial rescue party delivered him from the power of evil men, and his agony was not mitigated by any superhuman anaesthetic. We can only guess what frightful anguish of mind and spirit wrung from him the terrible words, 'My God, my God, what hast thou forsaken me?' But the cry 'It is finished!' cannot be one of despair. It does not even mean 'It is all over'. It means 'It has been completed' — and the terrifying task of doing God's will to the bitter end had been fully and finally accomplished.

J. B. Phillips

73   If Jesus was born today

If Jesus was born today
Would he come in the same way?
Would he be kind and heal the blind?
Or would he make them pay?
Would he be a rock star
or maybe an artist?
Or would he get married and settle
down in a big house?
If Jesus was around do you
think people might notice him and
listen to him or just walk away
and think he is dumb?

Paul Carrigan, 11 years

74 For thine is the kingdom
the power and the glory.

Hallowed be thy name, then
thou who art nameless.

Give me, oh give me
besides my daily bread
my kingdom, my power, and my glory.

All things that turn to thee
have their kingdom, their power and their glory.
Like the kingdom of the nightingale at twilight
whose power and glory I have often heard and felt.

Like the kingdom of the fox in the dark
yapping in his power and his glory
which is death to the goose.

Like the power and the glory of the goose in the mist
honking over the lake.

And I, a naked man, calling
calling to thee for my manna,
my kingdom, my power, and my glory.

D. H. Lawrence

75 **Then will he come**

When through the whirl of wheels, and engines
  humming,
  Patiently powerful for the sons of men,
Peals like a trumpet promise of his coming
  Who in the clouds is pledged to come again;

When through the night the furnace fires a-flaring,
  Shooting out tongues of flame like leaping blood,
Speak to the heart of Love, alive and daring,
  Sing of the boundless energy of God;

When in the depths the patient miner striving
  Feels in his arms the vigour of the Lord,
Strikes for a kingdom and his King's arriving,
  Holding his pick more splendid than the sword;

When on the sweat of labour and its sorrow,
    Toiling in twilight flickering and dim,
Flames out the sunshine of the great tomorrow,
    When all the world looks up because of him —

Then will he come with meekness for his glory,
    God in a workman's jacket as before,
Living again the eternal gospel story,
    Sweeping the shavings from his workshop floor.

G. A. Studdert Kennedy

76   Walking on water looks difficult,
    but I have seen it done.

Those with enough grief to sink them
have kept on —
drawn by an invisible source
of strength
they were not let down.

Crossing this sea
some swim
and others drown,
but some there are
walking on water.

Cecily Taylor

77   The Lord is my pace-maker
        Deep within he sets the pattern,
        The limits of the possible.
        At his rate I unfold.
        Through the demands of the world
        And its people around me
        He stimulates the lazy heart.
        Through routine living,
        Eating this day's bread,
        He soothes and stabilises it.

        He is the maker, creator of order,
        In the worlds of my body,
        Of nature, of man.
        He is the maker, brings poetry of vision
        Outside our structured
        Ways of knowing.
        Both mysteries are his.

        I cannot step outside his governance.
        For if I try,
        And seek my pace, not his,
        He sets the price that I shall pay,
        And at his time I pay it.

        In some measure of his pace
        Must I abide,
        There is no other.
        But he gives me choice
        How I shall know my life.
        He has many paces
        In his peace.

        W. S. Beattie

78   The Lord is my Pace Setter — I shall not rush —
     He makes me stop for quiet intervals.
     He provides me with images of stillness which restore my
         serenity.
     He leads me in ways of efficiency through calmness of mind
     And his guidance is Peace.

     Even though I have a great many things to accomplish
         each day,
     I will not fret,
     For his presence is here.
     His kindness now, his all-importance, will keep me in
         balance.
     He prepares refreshment and renewal in the midst of my
         activity.
     By anointing my mind with his oils of tranquillity,
     My cup of joyous energy overflows.
     Truly harmony and effectiveness shall be the fruits of my
         hours,
     For I shall work in the pace of my Lord
     And dwell in his house for ever.

     Anon (Japanese writer)

79   He was like a powerful current of fresh air that made us
     stretch ourselves and take deep breaths; like a beam of light
     that pierced the darkness and removed the scales from our
     eyes; like a whirlwind that upset many things, but most of
     all the working of people's minds. He did not descend from
     the top; he seemed to emerge from the millions of India,
     speaking their language and incessantly drawing attention
     to them and their appalling condition.

     Jawaharlal Nehru, writing about Gandhi

80   There are not two separate and distinct natures in Jesus,
the divine and the human, as the Church has maintained
since the final articulation of the concept at the Council of
Chalcedon in 451. The modern depth-psychological
perception of the inviolable psychosomatic unity of human
personality will not allow such a dichotomy. There was
only one nature — the human — but this was shot through
with the divine element which consists of what man has it
in him to become, the new man, the second Adam, the son
of man. Human nature is itself evolving, realising gradually
more of its divine potential.

John Yungblut

81   **What do people live for?**

I asked him once, 'Grandpa, what do people live for?'
    'They live for something better to come, my friend. Let's
say, there are cabinet-makers. They live on, and all of them
are just trash. But one day a cabinet-maker is born — such
a cabinet-maker as had never been seen on this earth —
there's no equal to him — he outshines everybody.
    'The whole cabinet-making trade is changed by him —
and in one jump it moves twenty years ahead. Likewise all
the rest — locksmiths, say — cobblers and other working
people — and peasants, too — and even the masters — they
all live for something better to come.
    'They live a hundred — and maybe more years for a
better man. Everybody, my friend, lives for something
better to come.
    'That's why we have to be considerate of every man —
Who knows what's in him, why he was born, and what he
can do? Maybe he was born for our good fortune — for our
greater benefit.
    'And most especially we have to be considerate of
youngsters. Kids need plenty of elbow room. Don't
interfere with their life. Be kind to them.'

Maksim Gor'ky

82   Our true mother, Jesus

A mother's caring is the closest, nearest and surest for it is the truest. This care never might nor could nor should be done fully except by him alone.

As we know, our own mother bore us only into pain and dying. But our true mother Jesus, who is all love, bears us into joy and endless living. Blessed may he be!

A mother feeds her child with her milk, but our beloved mother Jesus feeds us with himself. In tender courtesy he gives us the Blessed Sacrament, the most treasured food of life.

I dare to say full surely, and we should believe it, that there never was so fair a man as he, until his brightness was clouded by trouble and sorrow, Passion and death.

Lady Julian of Norwich

83   A meditation

God has created me to do him some definite service. He has committed some work to me which he has not committed to another. I have my mission. I may never know it in this world, but I shall be told it in the next.

I am a link in the chain, a bond of connection between persons. He has not created me for naught.

I shall do good. I shall do his work. I shall be an angel of peace, a preacher of truth in my own place, while not intending it, if I do but keep his commandments.

Therefore will I trust him. Wherever, whatever I am, I can never be thrown away. If I am in sickness, my sickness may serve him; in perplexity, my perplexity may serve him; if I am in sorrow, my sorrow may serve him.

He does nothing in vain. He knows what he is about. He may take away my friends, he may throw me among strangers. He may make me feel desolate, make my spirits sink, hide my future from me . . . still . . . he knows what he is about.

Cardinal Newman

84 Worship

Worship is the submission of all our nature to God.
It is the quickening of conscience by his holiness;
the nourishment of mind with his truth;
the purifying of the imagination by his beauty;
the opening of the heart to his love;
and the surrender of will to his purpose.

William Temple

85 A prayer

I am open to you, Lord.
Every nook and cranny,
every corner
of my life
Is yours —
open to your
penetrating eye.
And from my life
your hand
is flicking
The dust of indifference.
It had settled, Lord
and I am blind
to its presence
Until your light shines.

But come, Lord
and write
Your name in the dust
and let the tarnished vessel
show through;
And then,
when the dust has gone
Polish me with
Your righteousness
that I may truly
reflect your image.

Susan Appleby

86

Far in the distance, on the other side of the site, the sun,
red and enormous, was rising in haze, its beams cutting
obliquely through the gates, the whole building-site and
the fence. Aloysha, who was standing next to Shukhov,
gazed at the sun, and looked happy, a smile on his lips.
What had he to be happy about? His cheeks were sunken,
he lived strictly on his rations, he earned nothing. He spent
all his Sundays muttering with the other Baptists. They
shed the hardships of camp life like water off a duck's back.

Alexander Solzhenitsyn
from 'One day in the life of Ivan Denisovitch'

87   Here is a pair of hands.
And here
Within the Martha church
Are things to do, time-honoured, recognised.
And these are good,
They bind us to a fellowship of service,
Give us stability, a place, a limit,
A defence against the vastness
That else might overwhelm.
Take on this discipline,
Accept its irksomeness,
Or else who knows
What labour of Prometheus
Might swallow you.
Or else you might be lost
Living within a formless void
Perplexed to choose and purposeless.
Rest yourself here
In useful labour.
Occupy the time.
But do not doubt
That in the end all limits fail.
Be glad to know
That even here the wind may blow.

W. S. Beattie

88   It is not the critic who counts; not the man who points out
how the strong man stumbled, or how the doer of deeds
could have done better. The credit belongs to the man who
is actually in the arena; whose face is marred by sweat and
blood; who strives valiantly; errs and comes short again and
again; who knows the great enthusiasms, the great
devotions, and spends himself in a worthy cause; who at the
best knows in the end the triumph of high achievement;
and who at the worst, if he falls at least fails while daring
greatly; so that his place shall never be with those cold and
timid souls who know neither victory nor defeat.

Theodore Roosevelt

89   We are transmitters —

As we live, we are transmitters of life.
And when we fail to transmit life, life fails to flow through
    us.

That is part of the mystery of sex, it is a flow onwards.
Sexless people transmit nothing.

And if, as we work, we can transmit life into our work,
life, still more life, rushes into us to compensate, to be
    ready
and we ripple with life through the days.

Even if it is a woman making an apple dumpling, or a man
    a stool,
if life goes into the pudding, good is the pudding,
good is the stool,
content is the woman, with fresh life rippling into her,
content is the man.

Give, and it shall be given unto you
is still the truth about life.
But giving life is not so easy.
It doesn't mean handing it out to some mean fool, or
    letting the living dead eat you up.
It means kindling the life-quality where it was not,
even if it's only in the whiteness of a washed pocket-
    handkerchief.

D. H. Lawrence

90   I asked God for strength that I might achieve;
I was made weak that I might learn humbly to obey.

I asked for help that I might do greater things;
I was given infirmity that I might do better things.

I asked for riches that I might be happy;
I was given poverty that I might be wise.

I asked for power that I might have the praise of others;
I was given weakness that I might feel the need of God.

I asked for all things that I might enjoy life;
I was given life that I might enjoy all things.

I got nothing that I asked for — but everything I'd hoped
for.
My unspoken prayers were answered. I am among all men
most richly blessed!

An unknown soldier of the 19th century

91   It is true that missionaries have difficulties to encounter;
but what great enterprise was ever accomplished without
difficulty? For my part I have never ceased to rejoice that
God has appointed me to such an office. People talk of the
sacrifice I have made in spending so much of my time in
Africa. Can that be called a sacrifice which simply paid
back a small part of a great debt? It is emphatically no
sacrifice. I know that in a few years I shall be cut off in that
country. Do you carry on the work which I have begun. I
leave it with you!

David Livingstone

92   Safety is not behind but before, and the demand which
should ring ever more loudly in our ears is to enquire more
earnestly, more humbly, more patiently, more utterly in
the spirit of love and with a more exclusive regard to the
interests of truth. So shall we follow him who is True and
see the glory of his Kingdom which is Love.

John Oman

93   The sin of Pilate,
        Cowardice and political time-serving.
    The sin of Caiaphas,
        Spiritual pride and ecclesiastical time-serving.
    The sins of the soldiers,
    And of the crowd,
        Brutality.
        The lust for blood,
        And blind following the majority.

    These sins are not museum specimens, impaled on pins in
        glass cases, to be examined at leisure by those
        interested in religion.
    Strange reactions of long ago people
    In far away places.

    No. Far from it. They are the sins
    Of Acacia Avenue and Laburnum Grove;
    Neat, semi-detached sins
    Of respectable citizens
    Living in respectable rows.
    The sins of the milkman
    And the neighbour who borrows your mower,
    And the man who sits next you on the eight-fifteen.
    The sins of ordinary people,
    Going daily to ordinary jobs,
    And returning by six
    To unspectacular homes and wives.
    Your sins and my sins.
    The sins of the children
    Of our various parents.
    The sins of the man in your shaving mirror.

    It is these,
    The penny-plain treacheries of John Citizen
    And his unglamorous wife,
    Which flame in the heat of the moment,
    And flare to the sudden murder of God.

    P. W. Turner

94   Serving Christ in one another

You told us
to wash
each other's feet, Lord
as you did.

Did you not know
that we would
have baths —
wear closed shoes —
drive cars —
have metalled roads, Lord?

You opened
deaf ears
blind eyes
bowed
proud hearts —
I hear, Lord
I see
and give myself
to you
in washing others' feet.

On my knees
on their behalf, Lord —
Praying.
Too low
to judge
to criticise.
Vulnerable
to kicks
Vulnerable
to hurt
Vulnerable . . .

But that is what love is, Lord —
pride goes
self goes
fear goes —
and I learn
to serve you.

Susan Appleby

95   Passover lightly

'I have longed with great longing to eat this Passover with you,' said Jesus to his disciples; and they fidgeted and moved about and grumbled that the couches were hard.

Jesus began on the words of the Passover and ears were cocked critically: would these be the traditional words or the new-fangled Alternative Seder Book?

'This is my body,' said Jesus, 'which is for you'; but one of his congregation lolled forward and had gone to sleep.

'This is the New Covenant,' said Jesus, 'sealed by my blood.' And some said, this wine tastes bitter; others, it's too sweet — the service is quite spoiled.

Judas came to make his excuses: he had to leave early — something important, a business meeting, a rather vital little deal involving a piece of land called Blood Acre. Now Judas was the treasurer, and some of the others assumed he was off to do late shopping and began to think of purchases they should have made. But others thought he would be taking a gift to charity. I bet he'll give it to those zealots, they muttered; our money buying daggers for guerrillas!

'My blood is poured out that the sins of many may be forgiven,' said Jesus. I ask you, thought the disciples though they didn't say anything, what is all this theological stuff? Why can't he let us have it in simple terms? And all this emphasis on Sin. I'm not a sinner, I am proud to say (if you don't count fiddling the taxman and hating the Romans, and no reasonable man can blame me for that).

'Let us conclude by singing the "Hallel".' Oh hell, they muttered — that's the wrong tune he's singing.

'Thank you for your message,' said the disciples as they filed past Jesus (including the disciple who had slept through it all). But he knew what was in the hearts of men and he heard them say: but the seats were hard and so was the sermon, the wine was off and so was the hymn-tune. It's a good job we are churchmen, heaven knows what the man in the street would have made of it.

And they went out.

And it was night.

Peter Chave

96   Shall I betray him?

Shall I tell the Romans?
Or shall I not?
If I do
There will be money — quite a lot.

I'll give it to the poor
Like Jesus said I should
He'll be pleased no doubt.
Yes! I think I could.

Let him prove he's the Son of God
By saving himself from the cross
Then they won't bother him
And they'll see who's boss.

Yes! I will tell the Romans
There's no doubt about that
After the Passover supper
So Jesus won't smell a rat.

Samantha Milton, 11 years
Rebecca Morely, 11 years

97   The Keys of the Kingdom

No frame,
No frame can hold it.
Chaos.
Colour Chaos.
Caused by Eve
Lifting her hand
To take an apple.
In the chaos
A golden box
The Life of Christ.
Lined with Cross wood
It contains three Nails.
These Nails
Are the Keys of the Kingdom.

Sister Sarah Magdalene

98   What is the use of words?
Consider these
(We've heard them many, many times)
That 'God' so 'loved' the world
That he 'gave' his 'only-begotten Son'
That whoso 'believeth in him'
Shall have 'everlasting life'.
These words hold truth.
These words are quite inadequate.
These words are almost inaccessible.
But these are all we have.

W. S. Beattie

99   **John 3.16**

In the light of evolution and the revelation of depth-psychological insights the new lines of the Christ-myth will assume a form something like this: God so loved the world that he implanted deep within matter itself the promise of the Christ-life, to the end that in the course of continuing creation through evolution it would one day flower in Jesus of Nazareth, thereby quickening the same Christ-life in others to the eventual rise of the new man on earth.

John Yungblut

100   Christ on the cross,
Not crushed by death,
But broken by his love too deep for knowing;
Christ on the cross,
Not crushed by death,
But living on in love too deep for crushing.

Christ on the cross,
Not slain for sin,
But broken by his love too great for giving;
Christ on the cross,
Not crushed by death,
But living on in love too great for slaying.

Christ on the cross,
Not killed by man,
But broken by his love too strong for holding;
Christ on the cross,
Not crushed by death,
But living on in love too strong for killing.

Clare Richards

101   is it possible
for a man to speak
to another man's heart?
for a man on
a cross
2000 years
upon a hill
to speak
today to
a man's own
heart?
is it possible
for one man's
death
to be another
man's life
when that man's
death
2000 years
upon a hill
said death
to his friends
and desolation
to his mother?
is it possible
for one man's
shadow to
throw light
on life and love
2000 years?

is it?

Anon

102   Two voices

Good Friday

Without listening,
Without knowing it,
The Lost man said:
'Give me a dead tree,
A green hill
With a hole in it;
A handful of nails,
Old rope;
A bag of spite,
Blanket of apathy,
A crate of cowardice;
Full spate of hate
And fear, a pinch
Of expediency —
And I will put out
The Light of Life
For ever.'

Easter Sunday

Fully persuaded,
The New man said:
'Give me one grain
Of faith;
One leap of hope;
One glance of love;
And each one
Pure, undiluted,
Genuine
As a diamond
Without flaw —
And I will banish
Death
And all his dominion
For ever.'

A. J. Lewis

103   Guardian of peace, shadowed on a cross to die.
Light feareth the cursed night.
A set picture of fear, engraved in the dark sky.
Bells ring his death . . .

But he shall rise, rise to the paradise,
Rise into freedom.

Helen Poore, 10 years

EASTER

Easter is about Jesus. It is also about us. Resurrection is discerned 'in the ordinary gritty routine of our daily lives'. Francis Kilvert can pinpoint a resurrection experience on Monday 24th May 1875, and W. B. Yeats 'in a crowded London shop'. What happened to Jesus authenticates these human experiences. They in their turn offer us a brief glimpse of what for Jesus became eternally true.

104 Easter

Does the word 'Easter' occur in the Bible? In the Authorised Version — yes, once (Acts 12.4), but in no version since then. It was really a mistake intended to suggest to Christian readers the time of the year. So 'Easter' is not in the Bible. And no wonder! — when we know what it first stood for. It comes from *Eostre*, and Eostre was, of all things, a pagan goddess!

In fact, special eggs were used; buns like our hot-cross buns, simnel cake, and decorations, all were part of a festival at this time of the year, long before England was Christian.

They were celebrating the Spring. Everything had seemed dead, dull and hopeless. Then, suddenly, there were green shoots, then leaves, then flowers. Who had caused all this? A god, of course — or rather a goddess, whom they called Eostre.

When people became Christian they began to wonder about keeping this festival. Surely it was pagan? But it *need* not be! It was just right for remembering the Resurrection. Everything had seemed dead, dull and hopeless. But not now. Jesus was alive again.

So they took the old pagan festival and made it Christian. They kept the old name, Eostre — but they dedicated it to Jesus. And so do we.

Source unknown

105   The churches loudly assert: we preach Christ crucified!
But in so doing, they preach only half of the passion, and do
only half their duty. The creed says: 'He was crucified,
died, and was buried . . . the third day he rose again from
the dead.' And again 'I believe in the resurrection of the
body,' so that to preach Christ crucified is to preach half
the truth.

It is the business of the Church to preach Christ born
among men which is Christmas, Christ crucified which is
Good Friday, and Christ risen which is Easter. And after
Easter, till November and All Saints, and till
Annunciation, the year belongs to the risen Lord: that is all
the full flowering summer and the autumn of wheat and
fruit. All belong to Christ risen.

But the churches insist on Christ crucified and rob us of
the blossom and fruit of the year.

The *resurrection is to life*, not to death. Can I not then walk
this earth in gladness being risen from sorrow? Is the flesh
that was crucified become as poison to the crowds in the
street, or is it a strong blossoming out of the earth's humus?

D. H. Lawrence

106   Christ is risen indeed, and goes before you into Galilee.

Your Galilee,
The Galilee of the modern industrial city,
Of the neon lights, and the multiple store,
Where you jostle Christ on the pavement
Among the plate-glass windows.

Galilee Street,
The street in which you live,
And where he waits to move in,
Fulfilling his promise to be with us,
Always,
Even to the end of the world.

Arise, shine,
Thy light is come,
And the glory of the Lord is risen upon thee.

P. W. Turner

107   If you believe that Christ has risen
   from the dead,
you must believe also that you yourselves
   have likewise risen with him . . .
and if you believe yourselves
   dead with Christ,
you must believe that
   you will also live with him;
and if you believe that Christ
   is dead to sin
and lives to God,
   you too must be dead to sin
and alive to God.

Origen

108   When we begin to recognise the power of resurrection
present in the ordinary gritty routine of our daily lives, then
we shall see for ourselves that all that separates and injures
and destroys is being overcome by what unites and heals
and creates. We shall no longer have to ask where and when
this happens, for we shall have first-hand experience of it as
we live as ordinary folk in the ordinary world. But what,
then, of resurrection as future, of resurrection as our entry
into the life of the world to come? If we have been aware of
resurrection in this life, then, and only then, shall we be
able or ready to receive the hope of final resurrection after
physical death. Resurrection as our final and ultimate
future can be known only by those who perceive
resurrection with us now encompassing all we are and do.

H. A. Williams

109   Christmas is really
for the children.
Especially for children
who like animals, stables,
stars and babies wrapped
in swaddling clothes.
Then there are wise men,
kings in fine robes,
humble shepherds and a
hint of rich perfume.

Easter is not really
for the children
unless accompanied by a
cream filled egg.
It has whips, blood, nails,
a spear and allegations
of body snatching.
It involves politics, God
and the sins of the world.
It is not good for people
of a nervous disposition.
They would do better to
think on rabbits, chickens
and the first snowdrop
of spring.
Or they'd do better to
wait for a re-run of
Christmas without asking
too many questions about
what Jesus did when he grew up
or whether there's any connection.

Steve Turner

110   One day, when my sufferings were at their worst, I was listening to the Seventh Symphony (Beethoven), and suddenly, as the woodwind announced the lovely, tranquil theme
of the Trio to the Scherzo, I felt the load drop from me, as
did Bunyan's Pilgrim before the Cross. 'Fear no more,'
said the Trio; 'fear no more! Underneath are the ever-

lasting arms.' The relief and reassurance were deep and sweet; and, although the cure had only begun, its power increased steadily. From that moment I could always recapture the renovating virtue by thinking of that Trio.

Basil Willey

111   Christ is the Lord of the smallest atom,
Christ is the Lord of outer space,
Christ is the Lord of the constellations,
Christ is the Lord of every place;

    Of the furthest star,
    Of the coffee bar,
    Of the length of the Berlin Wall;
    Of the village green,
    Of the Asian scene,
    Christ is the Lord of all;

Christ is the Lord of the human heart-beat,
Christ is the Lord of every breath,
Christ is the Lord of man's existence,
Christ is the Lord of life and death.

Christ is the Lord of our thoughts and feelings,
Christ is the Lord of all we plan,
Christ is the Lord of a man's decision,
Christ is the Lord of total man:

    In the local street,
    Where the people meet,
    In the church or the nearby hall;
    In the factory,
    In the family,
    Christ is the Lord of all.

Christ is the Lord of our love and courtship,
Christ is the Lord of man and wife,
Christ is the Lord of the things we care for,
Christ is the Lord of all our life.

Anon

112   *Monday 24 May 1875*
This afternoon I walked over to Lanhill. As I came down
from the hill into the valley across the golden meadows and
among the flower-scented hedges a great wave of emotion
and happiness stirred and rose up within me. I know not
why I was so happy, nor what I was expecting, but I was in
a delirium of joy; it was one of the supreme few moments of
existence, a deep delicious draught from the strong sweet
cup of life. It came unsought, unbidden, at the meadow
stile, it was one of the flowers of happiness scattered for us
and found unexpectedly by the wayside of life. It came
silently, suddenly, and it went as it came, but it left a long
lingering glow and glory behind as it faded slowly like a
gorgeous sunset, and I shall ever remember the place and
the time in which such great happiness fell upon me.

Francis Kilvert

113   When winter is around us, we cannot see the spring;
          But still we know,
          Despite the snow,
That spring will come one day.

With night-time's darkness round us, we cannot see
      the sun;
      But still we know,
      As shadows go,
That dawn will break next day.

When seeds are sown in spring-time, we cannot see the
      flowers;
      But still we know;
      Prepared below,
A flower will greet the day.

'Though God is all around us, we cannot see his face;
      But still we know;
      Our love says so!
God lives in every day.

Donald Hilton

114 My heart leaps up when I behold
    A rainbow in the sky:
So was it when my life began;
So is it now I am a man:
So be it when I shall grow old,
    Or let me die!
The child is father of the man;
And I could wish my days to be
Bound each to each by natural piety.

William Wordsworth

115 Once as I was looking at a calceolaria, fingering the yellow
blossom, marvelling at the mouth that opened and shut and
the bulbous under-lip speckled with crimson, God was
with me in the garden. It was a moment in time and yet out
of it, I wanted to prolong it. But I could not. It had passed
and I was alone.

Elizabeth Hamilton

116 My fiftieth year had come and gone,
I sat, a solitary man,
In a crowded London shop,
An open book and empty cup
On the marble table-top.
While on the shop and street I gazed
My body of a sudden blazed;
And twenty minutes more or less
It seemed so great a happiness,
That I was blessed and could bless.

W. B. Yeats

117   During the two years just before and after I was twenty I
had two experiences which led to religious conversion. The
first occurred when I was waiting at a bus stop on a wet
afternoon. It was opposite the Odeon cinema, outside the
station, and I was surrounded by people, shops, cars. A
friend was with me. All of a sudden, for no apparent
reason, everything looked different. Everything I could see
shone, vibrated, throbbed with joy and with meaning. I
knew that it had done this all along, and would go on doing
it, but that usually I couldn't see it. It was all over in a
minute or two. I climbed on the bus, saying nothing to my
friend — it seemed impossible to explain — and sat stunned
with astonishment and happiness.

The second experience occurred some months later. I left
my office at lunch-time, stopped at a small Greek café in
Fleet Street to buy some rolls and fruit, and walked up
Chancery Lane. It was an August day, quite warm but
cloudy, with the sun glaringly, painfully bright behind the
clouds. I had a strong sense that something was about to
happen. I sat on a seat in the garden of Lincoln's Inn
waiting for whatever it was to occur. The sun behind the
clouds grew brighter and brighter, the clouds assumed a
shape which fascinated me, and between one moment and
the next, although no word had been uttered, I felt myself
spoken to. I was aware of being regarded in love, of being
wholly accepted, accused, forgiven, all at once. The joy of
it was the greatest I had ever known in my life. I felt I had
been born for this moment and had marked time till it
occurred.

Monica Furlong

118   While we deliberate, God reigns;
When we decide wisely, he reigns;
When we decide foolishly, he reigns;
When we serve him in humble loyalty, he reigns;
When we serve him self-assertively, he reigns;
When we rebel and seek to withhold our service,
He reigns: the Alpha and the Omega,
Which was, and which is, and which is to come,
The Almighty.

William Temple

119   Methought that in a solemn church I stood.
Its marble acres, worn with knees and feet,
Lay spread from door to door, from street to street.
Midway the form hung high upon the rood
Of him who gave his life to be our good;
Beyond, priests flitted, bowed and murmured meet,
Among the candles shining still and sweet.
Men came and went, and worshipped as they could —
And still their dust a woman with her broom,
Bowed to her work, kept sweeping to the door.
Then saw I, slow through all the pillared gloom,
Across the church a silent figure come;
'Daughter,' it said, 'thou sweepest well my floor!'
'It is the Lord!' I cried, and saw no more.

George Macdonald

SPRING

Springtime interlocks clearly with human experience. The year is a growing child, full of promise. As spring is complete in itself, though it points to oncoming experience, so childhood is complete. There is a maturity of childhood as valid as, though different from, the maturity of the adult. Even if spring did not teach us this the life of Jesus would. His humanity was as well expressed by his childhood as by his manhood. 'Whether at ten years, ten months, or ten days there is the right relationship to God fitted to that age.'

120   Autumn has gone and Winter follows,
Snow lies deep in chilly hollows;
Clouds and cloudy shadows fly
Across the cold and stormy sky.
Frosty days grow ever shorter,
Knifing winds give us no quarter;
Briefer birdsong soon is done
As twilight drowns the dusky sun.
Cold white moon, curled like a feather,
Brilliant stars mean bitter weather;
And yet — while Winter rules as king —
The snowdrop spears speak daringly, of Spring.

Aileen Gee

121   **Streaming golden hair**

Streaming through meadows
Streaming over the hills
Streaming through the countryside
Are a million daffodils

Anneliese Appleby, 9 years

122   Nothing is so beautiful as Spring —
      When weeds, in wheels, shoot long and lovely and lush;
      Thrush's eggs look little low heavens, and thrush
    Through the echoing timber does so rinse and wring
    The ear, it strikes like lightnings to hear him sing;
      The glassy peartree leaves and blooms, they brush
      The descending blue; that blue is all in a rush
    With richness; the racing lambs too have fair their fling.

    What is all this juice and all this joy?
      A strain of the earth's sweet being in the beginning
    In Eden garden. — Have, get, before it cloy,
      Before it cloud, Christ, lord, and sour with sinning,
    Innocent mind and Mayday in girl and boy,
      Most, O maid's child, thy choice and worthy the
      winning.

Gerard Manley Hopkins

123   **The acorn**

    Here beside the hedge I stand
    With an acorn in my hand.
    Folded small as small may be,
    In the acorn lies a tree.

    If this magic thing I keep,
    The tree will always be asleep;
    If it were buried it would soon
    Awake, unfold, and see the moon —
    The gleaming moon, whose light would flow
    Into the tree to make it grow.
    If the tree grows, the birds will sing
    In its branches every Spring.

    Here beside the hedge I stand
    With an oak tree in my hand.

M. J. Martyn

124   Childhood

No real cares,
I am free,
Floating through childhood
Like a bird on the wing.
Life gets harder
But I am going to keep my childhood as a small thought
Seated in my heart,
A beautiful thought.

I saw the first blooms of spring
Through my own eyes, as beauty;
The trees set against the summer sky, as hope;
The whole countryside, as love.
These thoughts should help me see things through adult
        eyes,
As children's eyes.

Sian Bennet, 10 years

125   As for what you call your experience, I call it waste,
        diminution, decrease, the loss of hope . . .
For it is innocence which is full and experience which is
        empty.
It is innocence which wins and experience which loses . . .
It is the child who is full and the man who is empty;
Empty like an empty pumpkin and like an empty barrel
        . . .
There, God says, that is what I think of your experience.
Go, my children, go to school,
And you, men, go to the school of life.
Go to learn
To unlearn.

Charles Péguy

126   'Brainwashing' and 'indoctrination' are to be repudiated,
but this does not mean that the reasoned teaching of
Christian doctrine is to be left out; indeed, how could any
pupils be satisfied with an understanding of any religion
that did not include a careful explanation of its beliefs? But

the pupil is not a blank page upon which the teacher writes indelibly: he is a person who, however much he is assisted, must discover for himself whatever truth he eventually holds. The aim is not the production of adolescents who can give slick and correct answers to a series of catechetical questions but the development of adults who will continue to reflect seriously upon the fundamental problems of human existence and to arrive at the decisions which life calls for, both theoretical and practical, in a spirit of responsibility. Teaching must therefore be open-ended, not in the superficial sense that teachers and pupils should pretend that they start in any discussion from no point of view, no belief, no conviction, nor that the authority of the teachers, derived from their greater knowledge and experience is ignored, but in the sense that enquiry is genuine, search for greater understanding is always present, and a real coming together of minds, a pooling of thoughts and of evidence, is always desired.

Learning for Life

127   Jesus is the normal child in the sense that his childhood is normative. There is a pattern of human childhood in the childhood of Jesus. The essence of this pattern is not that 'Christian children all must be, mild, obedient, good as he'. The child Jesus does not tell today's children how to behave. But the childhood of Jesus does confer on human childhood infinite worth. If the humanity of Jesus was as perfectly expressed by his childhood as by his manhood, then it must be affirmed that there is potentially for every child, at every age, an appropriate Christian maturity. Whether at ten years, ten months, or ten days there is the right relationship to God fitted to that age.

When Christians seek to nurture their young into Christian faith, they literally do not fully know what they are nurturing them into. They only know the resources but not the use which will be made of them. What we pass on to our children is not the painting but the paintbox.

Child in the Church

128   In the early years of life the baby begins to make his own contacts with the world, after the sheltered life in the womb. His mother is the world to him. He must first get to know her, and can only pass through her to the world beyond. Until he is about two years of age she is the focus of all his experience, and therefore the world takes its character for him from his experience of her. We can lay down the fundamental principle that unless he learns from her what love is and learns in turn to love her, he is going to find it difficult, if not impossible, to understand later on that God is Love. In the measure that he builds a picture of the mother as bad, he will later see God as an enemy. If he develops a sense of insecurity, God will always appear to him arbitrary and unpredictable, now stern and cruel, now over-indulgent and willing to overlook any misdemeanour. He will fear God and he will try to cajole him.

On the other hand, if he has met the right kind of wise love from his mother, he will face the world with trust and confidence, even when it hurts him, for he will have learned from his experience with his mother that beyond the pain and the effort of work demanded of him there lies an even greater satisfaction. He will go on in faith that if he endures and trusts, there is goodness to be found. It will not be a stoical endurance by which he will live, for, just as his mother asked patience and effort from him, so he will see that God asks the same at a more advanced level, and he will know that he is not suffering and called on to toil because God's love has been withdrawn from him, but that these may be the very signs of Gods love. His mother's love has been a preparation for him to understand the character of God. She has in fact been mediating God's love to him.

R. S. Lee

129   The half-strong

Because you are weak
You've called us half-strong,
Thereby condemning a generation
Against which you have sinned
Because you are weak.

We have given twice ten years time to you
To make us strong;
Strong in love
And strong in good will:
But you have not shown us a Way,
That is sensible ('sense-full; significant')
For you do not yourselves know the Way
Because you are weak.

And you took back the 'No'
In order to spare your weak nerves,
And you said 'Yes'.
That is what you called Love.

We are half-strong
And our souls are but half so old as yours.
We are noisy
Because we do not want to weep for all
The things you have not taught us.

We would even like to believe in God, strong to the limit,
Who understands, who wants us to be 'good',
But you have not shown us any man, who is good because
    he believes in God.

An unknown young German

130   If a child lives with criticism
       He learns to condemn;
       If a child lives with hostility
       He learns to fight;
       If a child lives with ridicule
       He learns to be shy;
       If a child lives with shame
       He learns to feel guilty.

       If a child lives with tolerance
       He learns to be patient;
       If a child lives with encouragement
       He learns confidence;
       If a child lives with praise
       He learns to appreciate;
       If a child lives with fairness
       He learns justice.

       If a child lives with security
       He learns faith;
       If a child lives with approval
       He learns to like himself;
       If a child lives with acceptance and friendship
       He learns to give love to the world.

       Anon

131   And a woman who held a babe against her bosom said,
            Speak to us of Children.
       And he said:
       Your children are not your children.
       They are the sons and daughters of Life's longing for itself.
       They come through you but not from you.
       And though they are with you yet they belong not to you.

       You may give them your love but not your thoughts,
       For they have their own thoughts.
       You may house their bodies but not their souls,
       For their souls dwell in the house of tomorrow, which you
            cannot visit, not even in your dreams.

You may strive to be like them, but seek not to make them like you.

For life goes not backward nor tarries with yesterday.

You are the bows from which your children as living arrows are sent forth.

The Archer sees the mark upon the path of the infinite,

And he bends you with his might that his arrows may go swift and far.

Let your bending in the Archer's hand be for gladness;

For even as he loves the arrow that flies, so he loves also the bow that is stable.

Kahlil Gibran

132   For, as far back as I can remember anything, I was somehow aware that my parents lived under the same kind of authority as that which, through them, was communicated to me. I could see that my parents too behaved as though they, *even they*, were not their own; and had they behaved as though they were their own and might do what they liked and might ask of me merely what they liked to ask, their authority over me could not have had the character which I actually felt it to possess.

John Baillie

PENTECOST

The Holy Spirit is the Spirit of adventure and pilgrimage revealing truth and light. He offers the gifts of joy, love and freedom, and draws us into the community of the Church which he enlivens. The group of people we meet each Sunday never quite matches 'the Church of our dreams', but its friendship, worship and sacraments sustain our vision, statements of faith identify the point we've reached in our pilgrimage, and we only lose his presence when we 'raise up a God in the image of self'.

133 For my part I cannot sufficiently bewail the condition of the Reformed Churches, who are come to a period in religion and will go at present no farther than the instruments of their reformation. The Lutheran can't be drawn to go beyond what Luther say; and the Calvinists, you see, stick fast where they were left by that great man of God, who yet saw not all things. I beseech you, remember, 'tis an Article of your Church Covenant, that you be ready to receive whatever truth shall be made known to you . . . He charged us before God and his blessed angels, to follow him no farther than he followed Christ. And if God should reveal anything to us by any other instrument of his, to be as ready to receive it, as ever we were to receive any truth by his ministry; for he was very confident the Lord had more truth and light yet to break forth out of his holy Word.

Pastor John Robinson
to the Pilgrim Fathers

134   Shukhov went to sleep fully content. He'd had many
strokes of luck that day: they hadn't put him in the cells;
they hadn't sent the team to the settlement; he'd pinched a
bowl of kasha at dinner; the team-leader had fixed the rates
well; he'd built a wall and enjoyed doing it; he'd smuggled
that bit of hacksaw-blade through; he'd earned something
from Tsezar in the evening; he'd bought that tobacco. And
he hadn't fallen ill. He'd got over it.

   A day without a dark cloud. Almost a happy day.

Alexander Solzhenitsyn
from 'One day in the life of Ivan Denisovitch'

135   It's easy to be happy. All you need
Is to add up your assets: strength and health
(Well, more or less), a home, a life to lead,
An interesting job, sufficient wealth
To keep me comfortable, things to do —
Like books to read, a garden to be — well,
Not dug, but cultivated — one or two
Good friends, a voice, etcetera. To spell
My various interests and pastimes out
In detail here would take too long. But think
Of these, put all your discontents to rout,
Let all those fears and lacks and wants just sink
From consciousness. It's easy: just thank God,
Forget the rest. Except I don't. How odd!

W. S. Beattie

136   And joy is everywhere; it is in the earth's green covering of
grass; in the blue serenity of the sky; in the reckless
exuberance of spring; in the severe abstinence of grey
winter; in the living flesh that animates our bodily frame; in
the perfect poise of the human figure, noble and upright; in
living; in the exercise of all our powers; in the acquisition of
knowledge; in fighting evils; in dying for gains we never
can share. Joy is there everywhere; it is superfluous,
unnecessary; nay, it very often contradicts the most
peremptory behests of necessity. It exists to show that the
bonds of law can only be explained by love; they are like
body and soul. Joy is the realisation of the truth of oneness,
the oneness of our soul with the world and of the world-soul
with the supreme lover.

Rabindranath Tagore

137   So tell me, what is joy?
Much easier to say what it is not:
It is not something that you do,
Neither the satisfaction in the doing of it,
Nor yet the pride,
The glory of self-praise
That afterwards
Leeches its virtue,
Not the looking back
That says
Then I was happy.
None of these.
Joy lives in ordinary things
And people one encounters any day
As something added to transform them
With the perceiver,
Binding all together.
The state of joy irradiates all around.
It is so personal
It goes beyond the personality,
Frees personality
From bondage to itself.

It is not subject to our will,
As one should say
Today I shall be joyful,
For it is we who are at joy's command,
Not it at ours.
Its seat and dwelling-place
Is with the dancing of the morning-stars
Before the throne of God,
And thence it comes
Like a brief ray of sun
Into a shuttered prison-cell
To be our token
That all shall be well.

W. S. Beattie

138   Love bade me welcome; yet my soul drew back,
      Guilty of dust and sin.
But quick-eyed Love, observing me grow slack
      From my first entrance in,
Drew nearer to me, sweetly questioning,
      If I lacked anything.

'A guest,' I answered, 'worthy to be here.'
      Love said, 'You shall be he.'
'I, the unkind, ungrateful? Ah, my dear,
      I cannot look on thee.'
Love took my hand, and smiling did reply,
      'Who made the eyes but I?'

'Truth, Lord, but I have marred them; let my shame
      Go where it doth deserve.'
'And know you not,' says Love, 'who bore the blame?'
      'My dear, then I will serve.'
'You must sit down,' says Love, 'and taste my meat.'
      So I did sit and eat.

George Herbert

139   God made man to be free,
Free within the human family.
The Commonwealth of man is still his dream.
In Charter and in Constitution,
In Petition and in Pact.
He inscribes his faith
In Freedom and Equality.
Yet still the barriers rise
And prejudice is strong.
Fear and suspicion separate
And sever man from man.

Why does the dream delay?
Why is hope unfulfilled?
Man lacks the faith,
He lacks the faith of Christ,
Who lived out his belief,
Who, in a hostile world,
Revealed the potency of love.
By this one act he realised the dream
And bridged the gap that separated man from man.
The wall was down.
And Jew and Gentile,
Slave and free,
Were one in Christ.

So when men dare to love
They can release a power
That heals the sad divisions of mankind.
Where men give up security and home,
To help a backward people with their skills,
There hope is born.
Where statesmen patiently negotiate,
And sacrifice advantage and prestige,
There peace can grow.
Where prisoner kneels before the bullying guard,
Immune to provocation and to hate,
There love can heal.
Where men will venture on a hope
Of truth and goodness yet untried
And take Christ at his word,
There God can work.

Jim Bates

140 It's dangerous to walk alone,
You risk discovery of yourself,
Peeling the layers of the social man
To find still there, within,
The tangles of a raw and timid youth,
To find that things that happened years ago
Are real and present in the mind,
To see yourself and others with more sympathy,
Confess how vulnerable we are,
How human, very fallible,
And beyond price.

W. S. Beattie

141 When the Commandment, 'Thou shalt love thy neighbour as thyself', is rightly understood, it also says the converse, 'Thou shalt love thyself in the right way'. If anyone, therefore, will not learn from Christianity to love *himself* in the right way, then neither can he love his neighbour; he may perhaps cling to one or several other human beings, but this is by no means loving one's neighbour.

Whoever has some knowledge of men will certainly admit that he has often wished to be able to influence men to give up their self-love, so he has often wished that it were possible to teach them to love themselves. When the busy man wastes time and energy on vain and unimportant projects, is this not because he does not rightly understand how to love himself?

Søren Kierkegaard

142   That same evening they were walking along under the trees
by Nether Green. He was talking to her fretfully, seemed to
be struggling to convince himself.

'You know,' he said, with an effort, 'if one person loves,
the other does.'

'Ah!' she answered. 'Like mother said to me when I was
little, "Love begets love." '

'Yes, something like that, I think it *must* be.'

'I hope so, because if it were not, love might be a very
terrible thing,' she said.

'Yes, but it *is* — at least with most people,' he answered.

D. H. Lawrence

143   Sunday's the day for holy work,
For each to do his bit
To keep the church afloat.
To sing, give lifts,
Or count the offering
And deal with business
In between the praise.
To get the latest news,
To see who's there
And note the absentees
With speculation.

Here, week by week we gather,
Mingle the edges of our lives
And interchange a stream of words,
Appropriate sentiments,
The social lubricant.
Yet of that Word we seldom speak
One to another
In ordinary human talk,
As if he were a precious ikon set apart,
His life a puzzle that defeats us,
His gospel news gone stale.

Is it a charitable silence that we keep?
Or are our tongues held back by modesty?
Or are we naked and in rags
But too polite to mention it?

A loyal activism,
A stoic silence,
A life kept private,
These we choose.
This pattern we can cope with.
Only, just now and then, a word
Of someone who has searched and found
Or has been found,
A word of joy not quite impossible
Cracks open our defence
And thaws the heart
In brief emotion —
Inconvenient, not quite proper,
Especially in church,
But real and human
And perhaps divine?

W. S. Beattie

144 I have walked with people whose eyes are full of light, but who see nothing in wood, sea, or sky, nothing in the city streets, nothing in books. What a witless masquerade is this seeing! It were better far to sail for ever in the night of blindness, with sense and feeling and mind, than to be thus content with the mere act of seeing. They have the sunset, the morning skies, the purple of the distant hills, yet their souls voyage through this enchanted world with a barren stare.

Helen Keller

145 We dare to laugh in church,
We've got quite used to it!
But do we dare to cry?
Jesus had a place for both,
Who said,
The Sabbath is for man,
As is his church.

W. S. Beattie

146   This is the Church of my dreams —
         The Church of the warm heart,
         Of the open mind,
         Of the adventurous spirit;
         The Church that cares,
         That heals hurt lives,
         That comforts old people,
         That challenges youth;
         That knows no divisions of culture or class;
         No frontiers, geographical or social,
         The Church that enquires as well as avers,
         That looks forward as well as backward;
         The Church of the Master,
         The Church of the people;
         High as the ideals of Jesus,
         Low as the humblest human;
         A working Church,
         A worshipping Church,
         A winsome Church;
         A Church that interprets truth in terms of truth;
         That inspires courage for this life and hope for the life
               to come;
         A Church of courage;
         A Church of all good men —
         The Church of the living God.

         Anon

147   The church — every gathering of the church, everywhere,
         under every form — *remembers* that on a certain night its
         Founder said and did certain definite things, briefly
         reported; that on the same night he fell into the hands of his
         enemies; and that he suffered a violent death (for the
         broken body and the shed blood can mean nothing else).
         The memory of the church thus takes us back to the same
         point where we formerly dropped anchor on our journey up
         the stream of history — the moment of the foundation of
         the church, when its Founder 'suffered under Pontius
         Pilate'. All lines run back to that precise point, which we
         might date tentatively to Friday April 7, AD30. Not indeed

that the exact calendar date is either certain or important; other dates are possible between AD29 and 33, but it *is* of some importance that the church remembers an event which is actual, concrete and in principle dateable like any other historical event.

The remembrance goes back in a continuous chain. At every service there are present elderly people who fifty or sixty years ago heard those words spoken by, or in the presence of, men old enough to be their grandparents; there are young people who, it may be, will repeat them in the hearing of their grandchildren. And so the endless chain goes on. For nineteen centuries there has not been one single week in which this act of remembrance was not made, one generation reminding another.

C. H. Dodd

148 Sunday rest day

There in the queue Shukhov learned some news. Again there wasn't going to be a Sunday this week; again they were going to pinch one of their Sundays. He, like everybody else, had expected it, for if there happened to be five Sundays in a month, they gave them three and made them work the other two. Shukhov had expected it, but when he heard it a spasm of pain caught his heart: who wouldn't begrudge the loss of that sweet day? Though what they were saying in the queue was right: they knew how to chivvy them even on Sundays. They'd invent something — fixing up the baths, or building a wall somewhere, or cleaning up the yard. There were mattresses to be changed and shaken, bed-bugs in the bunk-frames to be exterminated. Or they'd have the idea of checking you with your photo. Or of carrying out an inventory: turning you with all your things into the yard and keeping you there half the day.

Nothing seems to make the authorities madder than zeks kipping quietly after breakfast.

Alexander Solzhenitsyn
from 'One day in the life of Ivan Denisovitch'

149   Playing for time

Arthur Miller's screenplay of this name tells of the women who survived Auschwitz because they joined the band (later 'orchestra'), and played while fellow-Jews were marched away and gassed.

The band's a recommended way to drag out dying —
Perhaps avoid it altogether: we
Must take to piping for the *danse macabre* — undoing
Tuneless cries of those who march away . . .

I know we're prostituting what we have. But seeing
We're all like children in the market place,
Spoiling and spoiled, unsharing, discontent, I'm saying—
Why accuse us when you as well would please

Your captors — and yourselves? This generation's playing
The same old snatches; for you're just as bound
(By systems, treaties, trading terms) as we — employing
The same excuses as to why you bend

Your faith's imperative. Two thirds of men now moaning
Exit-lines, go gaunt, as those who pass
Our pipes, and strip to skeletons. And what's remaining
Filters down to some primordial peace . . .

I see a cheap-jack penny whistle in your hand.
Your application is accepted. Join the band.

Kate Compston

150   What is this place where we are meeting?
Only a house, the earth its floor,
walls and a roof, sheltering people,
windows for light, an open door.
Yet it becomes a body that lives
when we are gathered here
and know our God is near.

Words from afar, stars that are falling,
sparks that are sown in us like seed,
names for our God, dreams, signs and wonders
sent from the past are all we need.
We in this place remember and speak
again what we have heard:
God's free redeeming word.

And we accept bread at his table,
broken and shared, a living sign.
Here in this world, dying and living,
we are each others' bread and wine.
This is the place where we can receive
what we need to increase
God's justice and his peace.

Huub Oosterhuis

151 Christian nurture is therefore very different from the inculcation of a fixed set of beliefs and a fixed set of rules of conduct (which is an idea one might easily get from looking at some older catechisms).

The Christian way is not something fixed and unchanging. A living way is not a way that never changes, but one which remains true to itself. The mark of a living tradition is not immutability but continuity. Christian growth is thus not a matter of simply taking over the tradition, or of swallowing what it offers us, but rather of *responding* to what is offered. As we grasp it, make it our own, it does something to us. But at the same time *we* do something to *it*, as we interpret it to meet our own needs, and as we put to it the questions which face us now. We become new people by walking in the Christian way, but the way itself is continually renewed by those who walk in it.

Child in the Church

152   The parish priest
       Of Austerity,
       Climbed up in a high church steeple
       To be nearer God,
       So that he might hand
       His word down to his people.
       When the sun was high,
       When the sun was low,
       The good man sat unheeding
       Sublunary things.
       From transcendency
       Was he forever reading
       And now and again
       When he heard the creak
       Of the weather vane a-turning,
       He closed his eyes
       And said, 'Of a truth
       From God I now am learning.'
       And in the sermon script
       He daily wrote
       What he thought was sent from heaven,
       And he dropped this down
       On his people's heads
       Two times one day in seven.
       In his age God said,
       'Come down and die!'
       And he cried out from the steeple,
       'Where art thou, Lord?'
       And the Lord replied,
       'Down here among my people.'

       Brewer Mattocks

153   I believe in one world, full of riches meant for everyone
                 to enjoy;
             I believe in one race, the family of mankind,
                 learning how to live together by the hard way of self-
                 sacrifice;
             I believe in one life, exciting and positive
                 which enjoys all beauty, integrity and science;
                 uses the discipline of work to enrich society;
                 harmonises with the life of Jesus,
                 and develops into a total joy.
             I believe in one morality, love,
                 the holiness of sharing the sorrow and joys of others;
                 of bringing together people as true friends;
                 of working to get rid of the root causes of poverty and
                 injustice, ignorance and fear;
                 love, the test of all my thoughts and motives;
                 love, guiding me; controlling me; assuring me of God's
                 forgiveness;
                 and giving me confidence under his Spirit's control.
             I believe in Jesus, and the Bible's evidence about him;
                 whose life, death and resurrection prove God's lasting
                 love for the world;
                 who combines in himself life, love, truth, humanity,
                 reality and God;
                 who saves, guides, and unites all people who follow his
                 way.
             I believe in the purpose of God,
                 to unite in Christ everything, spiritual or secular;
                 to bring about constructive revolution in society, indi-
                 viduals and nations;
                 and to establish world government under his fatherly
                 direction.

Students of the Indian National Urban
Industrial Mission Course

154   I believe that there's
      Still hope to live
      — not merely to exist.
      Somewhere in this
      Hopeless whirlpool of life
      — a hand extends to help.
      In these battered days
      You will find, if you search
      — one who has offered to
            mend.
      I know that somewhere
      In this canyon of despair
      — there's a place of relief.

      Somewhere in this
      Turmoil of confusion
      — a right path to follow.
      Within this world
      Of make-believe
      — a faithful friend awaits
            you.
      In this polluted time
      We lead
      — a hope to be made
            clean.

                              Anon

155   **The people's creed**

      I believe in a colour blind God,
      Maker of technicolour people,
      Who created the universe
      And provided abundant resources
      For equitable distribution among all his people.
      I believe in Jesus Christ,
      Born of a common woman,
      Who was ridiculed, disfigured, and executed,
      Who on the third day rose and fought back;
      He storms the highest councils of men,
      Where he overturns the iron rule of injustice.
      From henceforth he shall continue
      To judge the hatred and arrogance of men.
      I believe in the Spirit of Reconciliation,
      The united body of the dispossessed;
      The communion of the suffering masses,
      The power that overcomes the dehumanising forces of
            men,
      The resurrection of personhood, justice and equality,
      And in the final triumph of Brotherhood.

      Canaan Banana

156 I believe in God the Father of us all, who has given the earth to all people.

I believe in Jesus Christ, who came to encourage us and to heal us, to deliver us from the oppressors, to proclaim the peace of God to humankind. He has given himself to the world; it is among all people that the Lord lives. He is among us all, the living God.

I believe in the Spirit of God, who works in every man and woman of good will.

I believe in the Church, given as a beacon for all nations, moved by the Spirit to serve all people.

I believe that God will finally destroy the power of sin in us all and that humanity will share his everlasting life.

I do not believe in the right of the strongest nor the force of arms, nor the power of the oppressors.

I want to believe in human rights, in the solidarity of all people, in the power of non-violence.

I do not want to believe in racism, wealth, privilege, or the established order.

I want to believe that all men and women are equally human, that order based on violence and injustice is not order.

I do not believe we can ignore things which happen far away.

I want to believe that the whole world is my home and that the field that I plough and the harvest I reap belong to everyman.

I do not believe that I can fight oppression far away if I tolerate injustice here.

I want to believe that there is but one right everywhere; that I am not free if one person remains enslaved.

I do not believe that war and hunger are inevitable and peace unattainable.

I want to believe in the beauty of simplicity, in love with open hands, in peace on earth.

I do not believe that all suffering is in vain, nor that our dreams will remain dreams, nor that death is the end.

But I dare to believe, always and in spite of everything, in a new humanity; in God's own dream of a new heaven and a new earth where justice will flourish.

A creed for One World Week from Indonesia

157 If, as a result of some interior revolution, I were
successively to lose my faith in Christ, my faith in a
personal God, my faith in the Spirit, I think that I would
still continue to believe in the world. The world (the value,
the infallibility, the goodness of the world): that, in the
final analysis, is the first and last thing in which I believe. It
is by this faith that I believe. It is by this faith that I live,
and it is to this faith, I feel, that at the moment of death,
mastering all doubts, I shall surrender myself. I surrender
myself to this undefined faith in a single and Infallible
World, wherever it may lead me.

Teilhard de Chardin

158 O Lord, pardon me three sins.
I have thought you — who are beyond thought.
I have described you — who are indescribable.
And in visiting temples I have forgotten
that you are everywhere.

Anon

159 But now you put a question to me asking, 'How shall I
think about Him, and what is He?' And to this I can only
answer you, 'I do not know.'

   With your question you have brought me into that same
darkness and into that same cloud of unknowing into which
I would wish you to be in yourself.

   Through grace a man can have a great knowledge of all
other creatures and their works, but of God himself no man
can think. I would therefore leave all those things of which
I can think, and choose for my love that thing of which I
cannot think.

   And why is this so? He may well be loved, but he may not
be thought of. He may be reached and held close by means
of love, but by means of thought never.

   And therefore you are to strike that thick cloud of
unknowing with a sharp dart of longing love; and you are
not to retreat no matter what comes to pass.

Anon

160 A fire-mist and a planet,
          A crystal and a cell,
     A jelly-fish and a saurian,
          And caves where the cave-men dwell;
     Then a sense of law and beauty,
          And a face turned from the clod —
     Some call it Evolution,
          And others call it God.

     A haze on the far horizon,
          The infinite, tender sky,
     The ripe, rich tint of the cornfields,
          And the wild geese sailing high;
     And all over upland and lowland
          The charm of the golden rod —
     Some of us call it Autumn,
          And others call it God.

     Like tides on a crescent sea-beach,
          When the moon is new and thin,
     Into our hearts high yearnings
          Come welling and surging in —
     Come from the mystic ocean
          Whose rim no foot has trod —
     Some of us call it longing,
          And others call it God.

     A picket frozen on duty —
          A mother starved for her brood —
     Socrates drinking the hemlock,
          And Jesus on the rood;
     And millions who, humble and nameless,
          The straight, hard pathway plod —
     Some call it Consecration,
          And others call it God.

William Carruth

161   God, our father and mother

As truly as God is our father, so just as truly is he our mother.

In our father, God Almighty, we have our being; in our merciful mother we are remade and restored. Our fragmented lives are knit together and made perfect man. And by giving and yielding ourselves, through grace, to the Holy Spirit we are made whole.

It is I, the strength and goodness of fatherhood. It is I, the wisdom of motherhood. It is I, the light and grace of holy love. It is I, the Trinity, it is I, the unity. I am the sovereign goodness in all things. It is I who teach you to love. It is I who teach you to desire. It is I who am the reward of all true desiring.

Lady Julian of Norwich

162   The soul is at home in God

I saw that God rejoices that he is our father, and God rejoices that he is our mother, and God rejoices that he is our very husband, and our soul his beloved wife. And Christ rejoices that he is our brother, and Jesus rejoices that he is our saviour. These are five great joys, as I see it, which he wills us to delight in — praising him, thanking him, loving him and blessing him for ever.

He would have us understand that the noblest thing he ever made is mankind, and that mankind's full and perfect expression is the blessed soul of Christ.

Greatly should we rejoice that God dwells in our soul — and rejoice yet more because our soul dwells in God. Our soul is created to be God's home, and the soul is at home in the uncreated God.

Lady Julian of Norwich

163 The relevance of the father phase for the religious development of the child is immediately apparent when we recollect that all religions tend to think of God as Father, and Christianity in particular specifically enjoins us to pray to him as such. Not only children but adults are taught the Lord's Prayer, 'Our Father, which art in heaven . . .'

In what sense do we mean the title? As adults we explain it as an analogy or a metaphor, but quite obviously we first find a meaning in it from our experience of earthly fathers. The sophisticated theological argument that we learn what earthly fatherhood means from the Fatherhood of God is a misleading one. The truth in it is that when we have extended the idea of fatherhood from fathers in the flesh to God, we have brought new meanings into it from our experience of God, and these new meanings can be brought back to apply to our fathers in the flesh. This is a secondary step. The first step is to apply to God the ideas of fatherhood we have learned beforehand.

If a young child is taught that God is Father, he cannot avoid applying to him the ideas he has formed of his own father. These ideas belong to the very immature outlook of the young boy or girl. They are quite inaccurate as a realistic description of the father as other adults see him or as the child will see him after the lapse of sixteen years or so, or even after six more years.

It may be objected that the child will grow out of such infantile ideas of God. The answer to that is that a great many people do not grow out of such ideas about their parents, but bury the infantile images in their unconscious minds, where they exert a powerful influence on our outlook and behaviour. It is far easier to grow out of ideas about our real parents than to outgrow infantile ideas about God. One has only to read a few well-known hymns and prayers to see how they embody infantile ideas about God. If again it is argued that these are the kinds of ideas about God that we ought to hold, the answer then is that religion is a matter for infants and not for full-grown men and women.

R. S. Lee

164 Perhaps the root of the trouble is this: the habit of mind which makes us think of God as one item in his universe, as one object among other objects, in the sense in which, for example, a newspaper might declare itself as being for God, king and country, or a theologian might say that although he is interested in many things God is his chief interest, or a devout person might say that he gives so much time to his work, so much to recreation, and so much to God. Thinking in this way, God is conceived as one being among a multitude of other beings, who stands over against us and is this and not that, here and not there. I have called this a habit of mind. But it is not really an intellectual error, a mistake avoided by the more intelligent among us. Fundamentally it is a failure not in intelligence but in love. It is due to an insufficient apprehension of the charity which is God. And it is the very meaning of our self-inflicted exile from our home, and so from our fulfilment and our peace.

H. A. Williams

165 William Beebee, the naturalist, tells of a ritual through which he and the late President Roosevelt used to go. After an evening chat they would step outside and look up at the heavens. Searching with or without the aid of glasses until they found the faint spot of light-mist below the lower left-hand corner of the great square of Pegasus, one of them would recite: 'That is the Spiral Galaxy of Andromeda. It is as large as our Milky Way. It is one of a hundred million galaxies. It is seven hundred and fifty thousand light years away. It consists of one hundred billion suns each larger than our sun.' After an interval President Roosevelt would grin and say: 'Now I think we are small enough. Let's go.'

Anon

166 Confidence in God

Almighty God —
Spies, Harlots, Murderers
Wars, Hardship and Death
all had their place
in the obtaining
of the Promised Land
for your people

Life has so little changed
since then
and,
like players in
a game of chess
without a king,
we try in vain to make sense
of what we find.
Forgive us, Father,
for speculating on your ways

Help us
in the knowledge
that you may be found
in all occurrences of this life.
Let us
go forward undismayed
in the acceptance
of this truth
and,
in the security
of your love,
give ourselves to your service
and the furtherance
of your Kingdom,
keeping our eyes on Jesus
the beginning
and end
of our faith.

Susan Appleby

167   Creator God,
        With your feet I walk,
        I walk with your limbs,
        I carry forth your body,
        For me your mind thinks,
        Your voice speaks for me.
        Beauty is before me
        And beauty is behind me,
        Above and below me hovers the beautiful,
        I am surrounded by it,
        I am immersed in it.
        In my youth I am aware of it,
        And in my old age
        I shall walk quietly
        The beautiful trail.

        Navaho Blessing

168   **God's creative mind**

        What shall I do today thought God
        to himself while sitting in bed.
        I know I shall make a world
        and the water will be red.
        No! I've changed my mind the
        water, I think I'll make it blue.
        And no one shall know what I'm going to do.
        I will make the birds and the bees
        and the flowers and the trees and Oh what a
        wonderful time I'll have.
        There will be fishes in the
        sea and animals on land.
        Just think. It will be
        Grand.

        Angela Glease

169 High flight

Oh I have slipped the surly bonds of earth,
And danced the skies on laughter-silvered wings;
Sunward I've climbed and joined the tumbling mirth
Of sunsplit clouds, and done a hundred things
    you have not dreamed of.

Soared and wheeled and swung,
High in the sunlit silence hovering there,
I've chased the shouting winds along
And flung my eager craft through footless halls of air.

Up, up, the long delirious burning blue,
I've topped the windswept heights with easy grace
Where never lark or even eagle flew.

And as with silent lifted mind, I've trod
The high, untrespassed sanctity of space,
Put out my hand, and touched the face of God.

J. G. Magee
A second world war fighter pilot
killed on his first mission

170   Know then thyself, presume not God to scan,
The proper study of mankind is man.
Placed on this isthmus of a middle state,
A being darkly wise, and rudely great:
With too much knowledge for the sceptic side,
With too much weakness for the stoic's pride,
He hangs between; in doubt to act or rest;
In doubt to deem himself a god, or beast;
In doubt his mind or body to prefer,
Born but to die, and reas'ning but to err . . .

Created half to rise, and half to fall;
Great lord of all things, yet a prey to all;
The judge of truth, in endless error hurled;
The glory, jest, and riddle of the world!

Alexander Pope

171   There is a sin that is without forgiveness.
       What is that?
   The sin against the Holy Spirit of God.
       What is that?
   The coat of humility turned inside out,
   To raise up a God in the image of self —
   To build a working model of the Almighty from the blue-
       print of our own character.
   Look! Here is the god you have made, bow down and
      worship.

   Glory to man in the highest,
   For man is the maker of gadgets.
   Hail to the Unholy
   Who gives us —
   That which we wish to get.

   I am the god with the sorbo face.
   The Average Man!
   Behold and worship.

   O thou who makest no demands,
   Who winkest the tolerant eye
   At our adultery
   And understandest our great need
   To get rich quick,
   We worship and adore thee.

   I am the god with the indiarubber face,
   Your grandfather in heaven.
   Behold and worship
   My avuncular benevolence.

   Thou art the god who disguisest thyself
   As a vegetable marrow at the harvest festival,
   And as Santa Claus
   At the Kiddies' festival of Christmas.
   Thou art Mars, god of war,
   To whom we turn
   During the period of the national emergency.

   And when all else has failed
   Let us fall to our prayers.
   O Lucifer, son of the morning,
   Image of man on the mirror of God,
   We worship and adore thee.

   P. W. Turner

SUMMER

There is a point in summer's plenty, before the slightest hint of the first autumnal frost, when all seems well and the promise of life has been fulfilled. Alison Head (Item 176) uses blazing sunlight as a symbol of a just and peaceful world in which society is built on mature relationships. Relationships are explored in this section, especially in family life, but with the recognition that we have not yet met the needs of the lonely, the deprived, or handicapped people.

172   Who should we thank?

Who should we thank for plants?
And tiny garden ants.
For sun and snow
And for water
That flowers may grow.
For birds and bees
For flowers and trees.
The summer sun
And seaside fun.
I know who to thank.

Donna Slade

173   If chance can dance the dust afar
In myriad motions to a star,
If chance can mould with pollen gold
The silken seeds where lilies are,
If chance one daisy can unfold —
Then God the hand of chance must hold.

Anon

174   The sun

The furious fantasia of the sun
And its blossom inferno.
God created a burning throb
With its tremendous rays reaching
Us within eight footsteps of time.
At night it creeps along to hunt another world.
Its destiny to follow
Its ever lasting path.
God was very scrupulous about the burning Sun.

Aran George, 11 years

175   The sun

What is the sun
In the bright summer sky?
I must not look,
For the sun in my eye
Burning bright light
Will bring pain and tears.
Ever burning bright ball
That I cannot get near,
You are the sun,
Yet when you set
In a wintry sky,
Orange fiery and low
Sinking down and down,
I can look at your glow
Above chimneys and trees,
Mellow winter warm.
You are the sun,
Sun fire, the light
That we all know.
I'm feeling the warmth
Of your burning red glow.

Elizabeth Lindsay

176   Then I saw the earth blazing with sunlight:
      I saw children laughing as they learned the secrets of the
          earth
      From people who smiled as they shared their knowledge:
      I saw the world celebrating Carnival; black and white,
      Protestant and Catholic, Christian and Jew,
      All joining hands and dancing through the countryside and
          the city streets:
      I saw the streets a mass of colour
      Where people left their jobs and houses to join the fun:
      And then I saw people returning to jobs
      Where they felt the fulfilment of creation:
      I saw faces full of peace and joy:
      I saw children full of food and excitement:
      I saw prisons with open doors for people to come out,
      And I saw homes with open doors for people to enter in:
      I saw beauty at every street-corner,
      And heard music in every home:
      I saw people discussing religion in bus-queues,
      And politics in the tube:
      I saw babies on the knees of old men,
      While their parents danced:
      I saw green grass, free from litter,
      And trees full of birds.
      I heard people singing as they cleaned the pavements:
      I saw houses, strong and shining with new paint:
      I saw each family with a home of their own
      And friends to share it.
      I saw people free: to love and be loved, to give and to
          receive.
      I saw peace in people's hearts, joy in people's eyes
      And a song on everyone's lips:
      I saw dreams being dreamt
      And lights shining in the darkness:
      I saw water in the desert
      And fire in the mountains:
      I felt warmth in the winter-time
      And heard laughter in the rain;
      I saw a pound-note in the gutter
      That nobody had bothered to pick up.

Alison Head

177 Homes

My house is large,
My friend's is small,
Other people's are very tall.
Some are on stilts,
High in the air,
And some I know
Are down below.
Some are made of mud,
And others of brick,
Even wood,
And some are even
Thin little tents.
Houses are all over
The world,
All shapes
And sizes.
But none of them
Are the same.
Everyone has different ideas,
But each one is somebody's home.

Yvonne Deans, 11 years

178 I've made a home.
Why don't you come and see it,
Any time you like.

I'm sure it's very nice
But I prefer my own.
Come and see that instead.

But neither did.

There wasn't much on telly
So I went to bed.

Tomorrow is another day,
And anyone I meet
Had better watch it.

W. S. Beattie

179 Mums and Dads

Clean your teeth!
Yes, mum.
Go to bed!
Yes, dad.
You have to be up earlier!
Yes, mum.
Hurry up, you're late!
Yes, mum.
Julie, your breakfast is ready!
Yes, dad.
Stop fighting you two!
Pick up those toys!
Tidy your room!
Make your bed!
Shut the front door!
Mop up that mess!
Get your brother's slippers!

Won't they ever stop?

Julie Riley, 10 years

180 My Dad

I like to play
Football with my dad,
And for him to choose
Pictures for me,
And lots and lots of
Other things.
But there's one thing
I like the best.
It's when we go up to
the downs
And act like stupid
clowns when
My dad's team
scores a goal.

Gary Milton, 10 years

181   A humorous look at my family

I live in a family that's a little bit odd,
There are five of us in it and one crazy dog.
We live in Kew Walk at number 2,
The house isn't old, but it's not very new.

My sister is bossy, my brother's as bad,
And when they both argue, it makes me so sad.
My mum is a Christian and so is my dad,
He tries to act young, but he's far from a lad.

I have lots of grandparents who live far away,
We travel to see them just for the day.
One grannie can't walk she's got a bad knee,
But it doesn't stop her getting a very lovely tea.

All my relations are perfectly nice,
But there's something to tell and I won't tell it twice,
If you want to be happy and keep all your friends,
You will have to be kind until your days end.

To just finish off my family tree,
There's eight lazy animals and one of them's ME.

Susan Hawkes, 9 years

182   The long run

When my dad
Takes the dog
For a run
We have
A lot of fun.
   But
I have to take
   Big Steps
To keep up
With my mum
And my mum
Has to take
   Big Steps
To keep up
With my dad
And my dad
Has to take
   Big Steps
To keep up
With my dog.
In the end
   We run
But we have
A lot of fun.

Martyn Love, 10 years

183 When Adam delved and Eve span
Woman, no doubt, was less than man.
When Eve begins to delve as well,
How can folks Eve from Adam tell?
So Adam must his pride maintain
By boasting a superior brain.
But this false claim is knocked for six
When Eve goes into politics.
So what is left for Adam still
Except to steal and rape and kill?
Unless you think — and you'd be right —
That Eve and Adam in God's sight
Are equal partners in the strife
Of building up the common life.

*Rupert Davies, on the presentation
of a garden fork to his wife*

184 **Fifty words on sin**

Male and female created he them, and was pleased.
'Behold!' he said. 'Very good!'
'Disgusting,' said the man. 'Messy, too.'
'Pornographic!' said the woman. 'And he's lustful.'
'I'm sorry,' he said, 'but you'll have to leave the Garden.'
'Don't you worry!' they said. 'We're leaving of our own
    Free Will!'

George Target

185 All alone

Alone, alone
In a wall of stone,
All the love in this world has gone.
Now I'm in this wall of stone.

Cut off from people in the world
All alone, all alone in this wall of stone,
I hear the rushing of the sea.
I wish I was not me.

David Salter, 9 years

186 But someone could try

When my mam married Ray,
All she would talk about was him all day.
He would sit and read the paper in the hall,
And he never had time for the park to play ball.
Then late one evening just before dark,
I left my home and went to the park,
Over the frost and over the snow,
Ray called to me but I said no . . .
He said he loved me but that was a lie.
All I could do was sit down and cry.
Nobody loves me, I heaved with a sigh,
No one at all but someone could try.

Joanna Elizabeth Lewis, 11 years

187 What makes a person?
Is he like an atom,
A billiard ball with its own colour
And character, that jostles and collides
With others, on the field of play,
But in it all remains himself?

Or is he like a meeting point,
A knot in a many-dimensioned net
Of roles, relationships and duties,
The sum of all he meets and does?

Or is he like a wave,
A complex rhythm
Passing through the world
And maybe resonating smoothly
Sustained by that around him,
Maybe in a jangle,
Heterodyne,
That rises to a peak of chaos,
Dies away in entropy?

Or is he all of these
And something more,
Beyond the resolution
Of our mortal instruments?

W. S. Beattie

188 . . . each person is unique, and created to the image and
likeness of God. Each then reflects God's beauty,
intelligence, power, freedom and love. We are all called to
be free, autonomous, self-determining, masters of our own
decisions. At the same time we are social beings, and
personal self-determination can be fully achieved only in
harmony with the social self-determination of groups to
which we belong.

Catholic Bishops of Australia

189 The death of John the Painter

John had a mental handicap which rendered him unable to communicate by normal means. He had remarkable ability to paint.

His twilight years have merged at last with death.
Stubby fingers no longer stab colour on paper
Yet there are so few who mourn.
A file is completed, a date recorded, a certificate written,
Officially a case is closed, neatly put away.
A handful of ashes, all statutory requirements fulfilled
And the bed in the corner sleeps a new occupant.

That brief flickering life
Drew from drab institutional walls
Such rich colours blending into ritualistic symbols
Must make us pause, shamed by our discontent.
A mind housed in a grotesque form
Conceived so much of beauty yet needed no words to
    utter
Yet no voice condemned our lack of vision.

We who knew him well remember,
Silently weep as we treasure those dream splashed
    frescoes
Screaming their message at those who pass by.

Only now, when John no longer sits
Crouched over a table scarcely noticed;
Only now dare we wonder if the labels we pattern
Have any meaning
Or our scribblings any value
Posed against his concept of creation.

Elizabeth Marais

190 Carlene

Carlene is deaf, dumb and has a mental handicap.

How can I reach your silent world?
Words cannot teach, or smash the soundless barrier,
nor actions penetrate your dumb unreasoning mind.

Twice damned, you seek with gesture and grimace
for contact. Frustrated you revert to tears,
make sounds which conjure half-remembered fears
of ancient tribal ritual.

Your strange unmeaning words fall harshly on my ears
for they had birth in your unknowing world.
How can I hope to span the years
of long-forgotten instinct?

Yet some spark of my persistence touches you.
You smile, clutch my hand, cradling it to your cheek.
Your tears are gentler now, flowing freely with the joy of
    our first contact.
Slowly at first, your fingers learn to speak
words which unlock your silent world at last.

Elizabeth Marais

191 If

Written by a handicapped person.

If you can keep your head when all about you
    are patting it as if you were aged two;
If you can trust your limbs when others doubt you,
    accept help with good grace, not as your due;
If you can be content with your low earnings,
    while others round have so much more to spend;
If you can learn to conquer normal yearnings,
    to 'sublimate' and not go round the bend;
If you can walk in crowds and keep your balance,
    or talk with kings and not let speech be slurred;
If, when they praise some very minor talents,
    you can let your real achievements go unheard;
If you can keep your dignity on falling,
    get up and face the stars still with a smile;
If you can bear the welfare workers calling
    to tabulate you neatly in their file;
If you can face your limitations squarely,
    yet keep on striving to the bitter end;
You will be more than just a spastic,
    clearly, you'll be a miracle, my friend.

Anon

192   Kate

What do you see nurses
What do you see?
Are you thinking
when you are looking at me
A crabbit old woman
not very wise,
Uncertain of habit
with far-away eyes,
Who dribbles her food
and makes no reply
When you say in a loud
  voice
'I do wish you'd try'
Who seems not to notice
the things that you do,
And forever is losing
a stocking or shoe,
Who unresisting or not
lets you do as you will
With bathing and feeding
the long day to fill
Is that what you're thinking
is that what you see?
Then open your eyes nurse
You're not looking at me.
I'll tell you who I am
as I sit here so still,
As I use at your bidding
as I eat at your will.
I'm a small child of ten
with a father and mother,
Brothers and sisters who
love one another,
A young girl of sixteen
with wings on her feet,
Dreaming that soon now
a lover she'll meet;
A bride soon at twenty,
my heart gives a leap,
Remembering the vows
that I promised to keep;

At twenty-five now
I have young of my own
Who need me to build
a secure happy home.
A young woman of thirty
my young now grow fast,
Bound to each other
with ties that should last;
At forty my young ones
now soon will be gone,
But my man stays beside
  me
to see I don't mourn;
At fifty once more
babies play round my knee,
Again we know children
my loved one and me,
Dark days are upon me,
my husband is dead,
I look at the future
I shudder with dread,
For my young are all busy
rearing young of their own,
And I think of the years
and the love I have known;
I'm an old woman now
and nature is cruel
'Tis her jest to make
old age look like a fool.
The body it crumbles,
grace and vigour depart,
There now is a stone
Where once I had a heart;
But inside this old carcase
a young girl still dwells,
And now and again
my battered heart swells,
I remember the joys,
I remember the pain,
And I'm loving and living
life over again.

I'think of the years
all too few — gone too fast.
And accept the stark fact
that nothing can last.

So open your eyes nurse,
open and see,
Not a crabbit old woman,
look closer — see ME.

Phyllis McCormack

193 Reply to Kate

What do we see, you ask
what do we see,
Yes, we are thinking
when looking at thee!
We may seem to be hard
when we hurry and fuss,
But there's many of you,
and too few of us.
We would like far more
    time
to sit by you and talk,
To bath you and feed you
and help you to walk,
To hear of your lives
and the things you have
    done,
Your childhood, your
    husband,
your daughter, your son.
But time is against us
there's too much to do —
Patients too many,
and nurses too few.
We grieve when we see you
so sad and alone,
With nobody near you,
No friends of your own.
We feel all your pain,
and know of your fear

That nobody cares
now your end is so near.
But nurses are people
with feelings as well,
And when we're together
you'll often hear tell
Of the dearest old Gran
in the very end bed,
And the lovely old Dad
and the things that he said.
We speak with compassion
and love, and feel sad
When we think of your lives
and the joy that you've had.
When the time has arrived
for you to depart,
You leave us behind
with an ache in our heart.
When you sleep the long
    sleep,
no more worry or care,
There are other old people,
and we must be there.
So please understand
if we hurry and fuss —
There are many of you,
and too few of us.

Liz Hogben

194   The small boy

Screams, shouts, laughter and noise. I open the door and little boys from every corner run and stumble towards me. I laugh and am so happy to see all their eager faces — even the noise is welcoming.

Then I hear a slight, shy voice. I see him crawling forwards. Every part of his body is involved in the effort. 'Laura! Laura!'

A triumphant smile appears on his face as he reaches me, hugging my legs. I hold him in my arms — it is hard not to have favourites. The small boy cannot move his legs — in fact they are a handicap to him. The future seems gloomy for him, but he has the will to make something of himself. His back is hunched through the inability to use his legs, but he seems to ignore all his disabilities. His smile is haunting and bewildering. Behind it is a sadness for which there is no medical cure. Each day he struggles in his efforts to speak, to communicate — each little word is a success.

Sometimes, it is frightening to watch him — alone in his solitary world — I watch him silently. Suddenly another child runs towards him, hits him and runs off. The little boy looks puzzled and a tear creeps down his face as the smile fades. He sees me looking at him, laughs and continues with life, forgetting his anguish. I think of my own grumbles, my own fears — how small they are compared with those of this little spastic boy. He has a contentment within his compact world which I find difficult to understand. Hate is an unknown feeling for him — he expresses love for everyone.

The smile of that little boy will remain for ever in my memory. He has shown me what true affection really is — a little soul with a hunched back, useless legs and a few words.

Laura Lovestone, 16 years

195   The gardener

You sows your seeds in spring,
Pops them in,
Covers them over with old mother earth,
Waters them well,
And waits awhile.
Then soon they'll come
Popping up from the ground,
Lettuce and lupin,
Carrot and marigold.
So you've got to know
What's what!
So vegetables goes in the vegetable patch
And flowers in the flower beds, see.
Flowers are for looking at
Vegetables to eat.
By summertime the flowers is blooming,
And the veg is ready for eating,
By autumn-time the fruits is ready for picking,
An' seeds need collecting for planting next spring.
Yes, in the autumn plants tuck up for winter,
When old mother earth has her long cold sleep,
So I sweeps into piles the dead leaves as they fall,
And notice the nip in the air.
But for sowing your seeds just remember
You sows them in spring,
Drops them in,
Covers them over with old mother earth.
Waters them well,
And waits awhile.

Elizabeth Lindsay

196 I would have given the church my head, my heart. She
would not have them. She did not know what to do with
them. She told me to go back and do crochet in my
mother's drawing room; or if I were tired of that, to marry
and look well at the head of my husband's table. You may
go to the Sunday School if you like it, she said. But she gave
me no training even for that. She gave me neither work to
do for her, nor education for it.

Florence Nightingale

197 Old people funny
wrinkly as they are
sometimes mumble and groan
Funny
old people are.

Old people forgetful
forgetful as they become
they're very weak and need your help
Forgetful
old people are.

Old people stiff
stiff as they are
they need a hand up and have difficulty sitting down
Stiff
old people are.

Josephine Appleby, 10 years

198 Black is . . .

BLACK is my mother's loving arms,
BLACK is my father's hair,
BLACK is the deepest shades of night,
     that soften the day's harsh glare,
BLACK is the babe against my breast,
BLACK is the wild swan's wing,
BLACK is my love . . .
     and my loved ones . . .
BLACK is the colour of my skin.

Maureen Watson
an Australian Aborigine poet

AUTUMN

Harvest marks the beginning of our autumn celebrations but other events follow in quick succession. One World Week challenges us to a new sensitivity towards the victims of injustice and poverty. There is an opportunity to increase our awareness of human rights, and Remembrance Sunday calls for peace and a reconsideration of the meaning of patriotism.

199 Autumn resurrection

When the spent soil of summer yields to the turning blade
and the loose earth rolling tumbles in soft brown disarray,
a ground-swell in the garden recoils along the spade,
a gasp of glad relief quickening the stifled clay,
inspiring a soundless ecstasy of celebration.
  I draw involuntary breath,
greeting with empathy this autumn resurrection,
the rescuing flood of light and air dissolving death,
rejuvenating all with thrill of expectation.
  My palm I sprinkle with the earthy crumbs of power,
knowing here lies the most unlikely alchemy whence spring
a world of trees and heathered hills, fern, grass and flower,
the unpretentious cradle of green-growing everything.
  I breathe upon my palm,
enacting in this deed my kindship with the soil,
sensing the ancient plain-song of the primal psalm
of ground-swell in the garden and God-swell in the soul.

J. Emrys Davies

200 Not ours, O Lord, but yours;
The earth belongs to you.

We mine the copper, gold and iron,
We take the minerals from the earth,
Coal, wood, and water; soil and clay.
We use these gifts from day to day
But
Not ours, O Lord, they're yours;
The earth belongs to you.

From orchard tree and soft brown earth,
From bush and cane, from branch and stalk,
From rivers, seas and grinding mill
We take all good things as we will
But
Not ours, O Lord, they're yours;
The earth belongs to you.

We marvel at the swelling seas,
We gaze into the night-time sky,
By painter's brush or poet's tongue
We think they all to us belong
But
Not ours, O Lord, they're yours;
The earth belongs to you.

Donald Hilton

201 Refugees help us to see ourselves

Refugees are people not to be pitied but to be respected . . .
because it is the refugee who reveals to us the defective
society in which we live. He is a kind of mirror through
whose sufferings we can see the injustice, the oppression,
the maltreatment of the powerless by the powerful.

Melaki Kifle
Refugee Secretary to the
All Africa Council of Churches

202   I remember, I remember,
       The house where I was born,
       The little window where the sun
       Came peeping in at morn:
       He never came a wink too soon,
       Nor brought too long a day,
       But now, I often wish the night
       Had borne my breath away!

       I remember, I remember,
       The fir trees dark and high;
       I used to think their slender tops
       Were close against the sky:
       It was a childish ignorance,
       But now 'tis little joy
       To know I'm farther off from heav'n
       Than when I was a boy.

       Thomas Hood

203   *Thursday 15 September 1870*
       We were busy all day dressing the Church or preparing
       decorations. Mrs Price and Miss Elcox had got a quantity of
       wild hops from their fields and were arranging bright red
       apples for ornament. Also they had boughs loaded with
       rosy apples and quantities of bright yellow Siberian crabs.
       At the school the children were busy leasing out corn from
       a loose heap on the floor, sitting among the straw and tying
       up wheat, barley and oats in small sheaves and bundles.
       Gipsy Lizzie was amongst them up to her beautiful eyes in
       corn and straw. The schoolmaster, the boys and I gathering
       stringed ivy from the trees in the Castle Clump. The Miss
       Baskervilles dressing the hoops for the seven window sills
       with flowers and fruit. Mrs Morrell undertook to dress the
       reading desk, pulpit, and clerk's desk, and did them
       beautifully. Then Cooper came down with his men
       carrying magnificent ferns and plants and began to work in
       the chancel. One fine silver fern was put in the font.
       Gibbins undertook the font and dressed it very tastefully
       with moss and white asters under the sweeping fronds of
       the silver fern. Round the stem were twined the delicate

light green sprays of white convolvulus. The pillars were wreathed and twined with wild hop vine falling in graceful careless festoons and curling tendrils from wreath and capital. St Andrew crossed sheaves of all sorts of corn were placed against the walls between the windows, wheat, barley and oats with a spray of hop vine drooping in a festoon across the sheaf butts and a spray of red barberries between the sheaf heads. Bright flowers in pots clustered round the spring of the arches upon the capital of the pillars, the flower pots veiled by a twist of hop vine. Mrs Partridge returned from Worcestershire this afternoon and brought and sent us two magnificent branches of real hops from the Worcestershire hop yards. These we hung drooping full length on either side of a text Mrs V. had made, white letters on scarlet flannel, 'I am the Vine. Ye are the branches. Without Me ye can do nothing.' And from the corners of this text Cooper hung two bunches of purple grapes. Two texts in corn on green baize. 'Praise ye the Lord' in wheat ears, and 'Thanks be to God' in oats were placed over the doors, inside. Outside the great door branches of apples and pears hung over the door. The gates were dressed with ferns, fruit and flowers. Following the outer arch, within a border of Spanish chestnuts, oak and acorn, elderberries, barberries and apples, was Mr Evans' text in scarlet letters on a bright blue ground, 'Enter into His Gates with Thanksgiving'. An avenue of tall ferns and coleus led up the chancel. A row of the same plants stood along the altar steps, and dahlias were laid on brae fern along the altar rail bars. On either side of the entrance to the altar hung a splendid cluster of purple grapes, and along the rails were tied at intervals small sheaves of wheat and tall heads of Pampas grass. On the altar stood two sheaves of all corn with a paten between them worked in scarlet flannel bordered with corn and IHS worked in wheat ears. Above this hung a cross covered with scarlet flannel and adorned with corn barberries. On the window sill above stood a larger sheaf of all corn in a moss field and upon the moss lay all fruit, plums, apples, pears.

Kilverts Diary

204   You passed a resolution on the morning that I died;
You established a committee on the day my mother cried;
You deplored how the hungry of the world must waste
away,
How the refugee is homeless at the ending of the day.
Your voting was unanimous, you all gave your assent
To investigate my hunger on the day my hunger went.
My hunger went on the day that I died
And in my death your Lord was crucified.

You preached a brilliant sermon on the day I passed away,
As my soul went home to Glory I could clearly hear you say
How in Matthew chapter twenty-five it says to love the
poor;
Your three main points were all designed to make the
conscience soar.
Your diction it was faultless as you said just what you
meant;
But you preached about my hunger on the day my hunger
went.
My hunger went on the day that I died
And in my death your Lord was crucified.

But there are many like me who have yet a while to live
And you are not alone in having so much you can give,
Your sermons and committees will not take my pain
away —
You'll need a better tale than that to tell on Judgement
Day.
God lent you wealth to share with me, while to your
Government
He gave the power to save my life — the day my hunger
went.
My hunger went on the day that I died
And in my death your Lord was crucified.

David Goodbourn

205 Milking the natives

I never invited you
but you came to my island
and I welcomed you

You told me
I was a savage
and I believed you

You told me I was doomed to hell
and I was scared
you gave me your bible
and I prayed

You told me to till my island
I planted coconuts for your profits
You told me to dig holes and bunkers and
I defended you with my life and land
but you bombed my house and my land
and I ran into the woods

You told me
you freed me from your war
and I should be grateful
to you as my liberator

You established your government
on my island
without my permission

You sent me to your school
and I learned your way
and I worked for you as an office boy
you gave me your dollars
and I bought your things

Now you tell me
I cannot live without
your money
your way
your things
and I believe you

But I can only get them
if I give you my island and freedom
Never!!!

Moses Ymal Uludong

206   A Litany for the Day of Human Rights

For those who grasp their prison bars helplessly
   so that we may walk free — a thought.
For those who rot in the dark
   so that we may walk in the sun — a thought.
For those whose ribs have been broken
   so that we may breathe our fill — a thought.
For those whose faces have been slapped
   so that we may walk in fear of no hand — a thought.
For those whose mouths have been gagged
   so that we may speak out — a thought.
For those whose wives live in anguish
   so that our wives may live happy — a thought.
For those whose country is in chains
   so that our country may be free — a thought.
And for the jailers and for their torturers
   — a thought.
   The saddest of all, they are the most maimed,
   and the day of reckoning is bound to come.

Salvador de Madariaga

207

During my lifetime I have dedicated myself to the struggle
of the African people. I have fought against white
domination, and I have fought against black domination. I
have cherished the ideal of a democratic and free society in
which all persons live together in harmony with equal
opportunities. It is an ideal which I hope to live for and to
achieve. But, if needs be, it is an ideal for which I am
prepared to die.

Nelson Mandela
from his speech before sentence was passed
on him in the Riviona trial in 1963

208 Who will deny that thirty years of my life have been spent knocking in vain, patiently, moderately and modestly at a closed and barred door? What have been the fruits of moderation? The past thirty years have seen the greatest number of laws restricting our rights and progress, until today we have reached a stage where we have almost no rights at all . . .

Chief Albert Luthuli

209 **The preamble of the United Nations Charter**

We, the Peoples of the United Nations, determined to save succeeding generations from the scourge of war, which twice in our lifetime has brought untold sorrow to mankind,

and to reaffirm faith in fundamental human rights, in the dignity and worth of the human person, in the equal rights of men and women and of nations large and small,

and to establish conditions under which justice and respect for the obligations arising from treaties and other sources of international law can be maintained,

and to promote social progress and better standards of life in larger freedom,

and for these ends,

to practise tolerance and live together in peace with one another as good neighbours,

and to unite our strength to maintain international peace and security, and to ensure, by the acceptance of principles and the institution of methods, that armed force shall not be used, save in the common interest,

and to employ international machinery for the promotion of the economic and social advancement of all peoples,

have resolved to combine our efforts to accomplish these aims.

210   It will be spring once more

winter's coming,
summer's gone,
autumn's here,
but won't be long,
soon it will be spring
once more.

it had seemed
like years away,
when we left
our homes on that day,
refugees
for foreign shore.

we had left our dear land,
all its beaches and sand,
all its forests and streams,
all its hopes and its dreams.

will we see
our friends again?
all those mem'ries
will remain,
all our hopes
and joys and pain.

autumn leaves turning red,
naked trees stark and bare,
bracing hard times ahead,
soon the cold's everywhere.

winter's coming,
summer's gone,
autumn's here
but won't be long,
soon it will be spring
once more.

Francis Khoo Kah Siang

211 There is a freedom that man fears:
The freedom of his fellow-man
In the eye of the tyrant
In the eye of the oppressed
In the eye of the neighbour
Who makes his fence too high — or low;
In the eye of the traveller in the tube
Who, like him, eyes the seat he makes for.
There is a freedom that threatens,
That disturbs the freedom he has carved out for himself.
So we live
Shut in by fences, regulations, gates.
Apartheid in a thousand forms
Secures us from the freedom of the world
To invade and to destroy
Our liberty of isolation.

For freedom we build our walls,
For freedom we make our bombs,
For freedom we pass our laws,
For freedom we imprison and restrict,
For freedom we create the Ghetto.
And we shall meet no one,
And speak to no one,
And listen to no one,
Who does not look as we do,
Think as we do,
Act as we do,
Except at a safe and deferential distance.

For in our neighbour lies
The secret of our happiness.
He alone can liberate
The generous instinct
And dispel the fear
That shuts us in.

Jim Bates

212   Twinkle, twinkle, little star
I *don't* wonder what you are,
I surmised your spot in space,
When you left your missile base.
Any wondering that I do
Centres on the price of you
And I shudder when I think,
What you're costing us 'per twink'.

Anon

213   I was hungry and you blamed it on the Communists
I was hungry and you circled the moon
I was hungry and you told me to wait
I was hungry and you set up a commission
I was hungry and you said, 'So were my ancestors'
I was hungry and you said, 'We don't hire over 35's'
I was hungry and you said, 'God helps those . . .'
I was hungry and you told me I shouldn't be
I was hungry and you told me machines do that work now
I was hungry and you had defence bills to pay
I was hungry and you said, 'The poor are always with us'
Lord, when did we see you hungry?

Adapted from Matthew 25

214   Poverty is the moment in the world
When lilies and children
And all the things that matter,
Don't.
It is the moment when only bread
Is beautiful
Because it means another hour or two
Of living.
With only the hope that hope
Is round the corner,
No idea or solution
From a perfect flower.
Only live from day to day,
Avoiding death.
Don't give a lily to a man like that.
If he is hungry enough,
He will eat it.

Anon

215 Prisoners

In '41 Mama took us back to Moscow. There I saw our enemies for the first time. If my memory is right, nearly twenty thousand German war prisoners were to be marched in a single column through the streets of Moscow.

The pavements swarmed with onlookers, cordoned off by soldiers and police. The crowd were mostly women — Russian women with hands roughened by hard work, lips untouched by lipstick and thin hunched shoulders which had borne half the burden of the war. Every one of them must have had a father or a husband, a brother or a son killed by the Germans.

They gazed with hatred in the direction from which the column was to appear.

At last we saw it. The generals marched at the head, massive chins stuck out, lips folded disdainfully, their whole demeanour meant to show superiority over their plebeian victors. 'They smell of eau-de-cologne, the bastards,' someone in the crowd said with hatred. The women were clenching their fists. The soldiers and policemen had all they could do to hold them back.

All at once something happened to them. They saw German soldiers, thin, unshaven, wearing dirty bloodstained bandages, hobbling on crutches or leaning on the shoulders of their comrades; the soldiers walked with their heads down.

The street became dead silent — the only sound was the shuffling of boots and the thumping of crutches.

Then I saw an elderly woman in broken-down boots push herself forward and touch a policeman's shoulder, saying, 'Let me through'. There must have been something about her that made him step aside.

She went up to the column, took from inside her coat something wrapped in a coloured handkerchief and unfolded it. It was a crust of black bread. She pushed it awkwardly into the pocket of a soldier, so exhausted that he was tottering on his feet. And now suddenly from every side women were running towards the soldiers, pushing into their hands bread, cigarettes, whatever they had.

The soldiers were no longer enemies. They were people.

Yevgeny Yevtushenko

216 Lament

The blood-red petals fall.
A symbol of The Fallen
In useless wars,
Each fought to end them all.
'At the going down of the sun,
And in the morning . . .'
Have we remembered them?
Will the button-pushing fingers,
Flexed by grey and greedy men,
Demand once more a sacrifice?
The 'flower of youth' again?
NO! The present generation
Is made of sterner stuff —
And though the whole world bloomed with poppies,
It would not be enough.

Aileen Gee

217 Waste

Waste of Muscle, waste of Brain,
Waste of Patience, waste of Pain,
Waste of Manhood, waste of Health,
Waste of Beauty, waste of Wealth,
Waste of Blood, and waste of Tears,
Waste of Youth's most precious years,
Waste of ways the Saints have trod,
Waste of Glory, waste of God, —
　　War!

G. A. Studdert Kennedy

218 Let us open the clenched fist and extend the open palms
Let us mourn till others are comforted, weep till others
    laugh
Let us be sleepless till all can sleep untroubled
Let us be meek till all can stand up in pride
Let us be frugal till all are filled
Let us give till all have received
Let us make no claims till all have had their due
Let us be slaves till all are free
Let us lay down our lives till others have life abundantly.

Fr John Harriott

219 Peace is like gossamer —
vulnerable, yet indestructible:
tear it, and it will be rewoven.
Peace does not despair.
Begin to weave a web of peace:
start in the centre
and make peace with yourself
and your God.
Take the thread outwards
and build peace within your family, your community
— and in the circle of those you find it hard to like.
Then stretch your concern
into all the world.
Weave a web of peace
and do not despair.
Love is the warp in the fabric of life:
truth is the weft:
care and integrity together —
vulnerable,
but ultimately
indestructible.
Together,
they spell
peace . . .

Kate Compston

220 Peace is a young mother
Walking with her son
Hand in hand,
A smile of happiness
On her face:
And you knowing
You will not have
To meet her again in the street
Ten years later
Wearing black,
Tearful and wrinkled
A look of endless grief
In her eyes
Which nothing can console.

Peace is all this
For us and for other people as well.
All this and much,
Much more.

Shai Ben Moshe, 13 years

221 We built you a city and a tower,
A street we dedicated in your name;
Doves we prepared, trees and flowers
Woods and fields
But you — you didn't come!

Poems we composed, prayers, songs of praise
A story we wrote, a photo we took
And made a painting too —
But you — you didn't come!

We even made sacrifice
Life itself we gave
But you — you didn't come!

So tell me, tell me
What is it we haven't given you and we shall prepare it,
Shall offer and present it
Just say what, but come to us already —
Peace!

Nava Caspi, 15 years

222 I had a paint-box —
Each colour glowing with delight;
I had a paint-box with colours
Warm and cool and bright.
I had no red for wounds and blood,
I had no black for an orphaned child,
I had no white for the face of the dead,
I had no yellow for burning sands.
I had orange for joy and life,
I had green for buds and blooms,
I had blue for clear bright skies,
I had pink for dreams and rest.
I sat down
and painted
Peace.

Tali Shurek, 13 years

223 I don't like wars
They end up with monuments;
I don't want battles to roar
Even in neighbouring continents.

I like Spring
Flowers producing,
Fields covered with green,
The wind in the hills whistling.

Drops of dew I love,
The scent of jasmine as night cools,
Stars in darkness above,
And rain singing in pools.

I don't like wars. They end
In wreaths and monuments;
I like Peace come to stay
And it will some day.

Matti Yosef, 9 years

224   Peace, we will get you,
      Wherever you may be.
      Even though still a dream
      Today,
      We will get you, Peace.

      With flowers will we deck
      The gun barrels,
      And the young soldiers'
      Heads
      Cover with wreaths.

      Even if you be delayed,
      We shall not lose hope.
      We shall keep our fingers warm
      For you
      And there will be no more wars.

      We shall overcome every enemy with songs of Peace
      And the world will be quiet.
      Please, then,
      Do not run away,
      Wait,
      And let there be no more wars.

      Shalom Rufeisen, 14 years

225   If patriotism be a virtue indeed, it cannot mean an exclusive
      devotion to our country's interests — for that is only
      another form of devotion to personal interests, family
      interests, or provincial interests, all of which, if not driven
      past themselves, are vulgar and immoral objects . . . I
      confess that I dream of the day when an English statesman
      shall arise with a heart too large for England; having
      courage in the face of his countrymen to assert of some
      suggested policy — 'This is good for your trade; this is
      necessary for your domination; but it will vex a people hard
      by; it will hurt a people farther off; it will profit nothing to
      the general humanity; therefore away with it; — it is not for
      you or for me.' When a British minister dares speak so, and

when a British public applauds him speaking, then shall the nation be glorious, and her praise, instead of exploding from within, from loud civic mouths, come to her from without, as all worthy praise must, from the alliances she has fostered and the populations she has saved.

Elizabeth Barrett Browning

226 *Roger Schutz, better known as Brother Roger of Taizé, created a community following the purchase of a small house in Taizé in 1940. He tells of the early days of the community in war-torn Europe.*

As soon as he arrived in Taizé, Roger saw that the first task of the house was going to be a dangerous one. Only a few miles to the North lay the demarcation-line. Above it, even more than in Vichy-administered France, people were on the run, hungry, hunted and in danger. At every hour of the day or night Roger might see a refugee arriving at the gates of the house, sometimes people half-dead from exhaustion. 'I never asked them who they were. I would let them into the house myself; I had to do everything. I had at once begun to clear and cultivate the land, milking the cow myself too. I had a small chapel in the house, where I would go and pray on my own. I dreaded the thought that some of the guests might feel obliged to pray with me out of a sense of gratitude. If they were not Christians, that would have been a kind of violence.'

J. L. G. Balado

227 Be honest about violence . . .
how it thrills the blood,
enables men
to stand erect and act,
to exercise such power
and savage force
that rescues from
the cowardly and the trite.

Be honest about violence . . .
how it spills the blood
and tears through flesh
and nerve and bone and life,
destroying better sorts of power
and ways of life
and hurting most
the civilised and weak.

Be honest about violence . . .
how sometimes it helps
the victor and his victory;
and on occasion has been known
to help the victim too.
Be honest. Let
the victim judge . . . for once!

David J. Harding

228   The armaments factory worker

I cannot influence the fate of the globe.
Do I start wars? How can I know
whether I'm for or against?
No, I don't sin.
It worries me not to have influence,
that it is not I who sin.
I only turn screws, weld together
parts of destruction,
never grasping the whole,
or the human lot.

I could do otherwise (would parts be left out?)
contributing then to sanctified toil
which no one would blot out in action
or belie in speech.
Though what I create is all wrong,
the world's evil is none of my doing.

But is that enough?

Karol Wojtyla (tr. Jerzy Peterkiewicz)

229   If at any time they stop the radio, ban the papers, deny us the possibility of speaking, kill all the priests and bishops too; and they leave you a pueblo without a priest, every one of you must become a microphone of God — everyone must be a messenger, a prophet; the Church will always exist in the world for as long as there remains one baptised person and that last baptised person who remains in the world is he who has the responsibility before the entire world to maintain the flag of our Lord's truth and divine justice flying high.

Archbishop Romero of San Salvador

230   Behind this door there sits a man
Whose latent genius, if allowed to blossom,
Would rock the world;
Whose dynamic energy, if unleashed,
Would overwhelm all those around him.

Better let him sleep . . .

Anon

231   Communication

I am dumb,
   dead,
Tongue tied
   very dumb!

How can I communicate
So big a message!

How can pepper communicate the sweet?
How can failure radiate success?
The everlasting:
Will it go without mud?
I am mud, sticky mud!
Will I stick on the pure white?

But still
'Go and preach'
The Word tells me
The drums and the calabash
The birds of the jungle
All cry
'Go and preach
For God gave you power!'

Godfrey Lubulwa

ACKNOWLEDGEMENTS and INDEX OF AUTHORS

The compiler and publishers express thanks for permission to use copyright items. Every effort has been made to trace copyright owners but if any rights have been inadvertently overlooked, the necessary correction will gladly be made in subsequent editions.

Anselm, Sister Mary, 56 *More Wantage Poems* (A. R. Mowbray & Co Ltd), 68

Appleby, Anneliese, 34, 121

Appleby, Josephine, 197

Appleby, Susan, 85, 94 (first published in *Church of England Newspaper)*, 166

Badcock, James, 9 (first published in *Reform)*

Baillie, John, 132 *Our Knowledge of God* (Oxford University Press)

Balado, J. L. G. 226 *The Story of Taizé* (A. R. Mowbray & Co Ltd)

Banana, Canaan, 155 (quoted in *Now)*

Bannister, Sir Roger, 45

Bates, Jim,, 53, 139, 211 (Christian Education Movement)

Beattie, W. S., 4, 22, 28, 29, 47, 52, 65, 77, 87, 98, 135, 137, 140, 143, 145, 178, 187

Bennet, Sian, 124 *Simple Miracles* (Kelling C.P. School)

Bird, Amanda, 36 *Colours of Hope* (Kelling C.P. School)

Bonhoeffer, Dietrich, 21 *Letters and Papers from Prison* (SCM Press)

Boore, Michael, 48 *Colours of Hope* (Kelling C.P. School)

Brown, Michael, 25

Browning, Elizabeth Barrett, 225*

Carrigan, Paul, 73 *Something to Say* (Sheffield Diocesan Education Cttee)

Carruth, William, 160*

Caspi, Nava, 221 *My Shalom, My Peace* (Sabra Books)

Chave, Peter, 95 (first published in *Reform)*

Compston, Kate, 149 (first published in *Reform)*, 219

Davies, J. Emrys, 199 (first published in *Reform)*

Davies, Rupert, 183 *Circles of Community* (British Council of Churches)

de Chardin, Teilhard, 157 *The Teilhard Review*

De Madariaga, Salvadore, 206 (Amnesty International)

Deans, Yvonne, 177 (Horfield C.E. School)

Dodd, C. H. 147 *The Founder of Christianity* (Collins Publishers)

Furlong, Monica, 117 *Travelling In* (Anthony Shiel Associates Ltd)

Garry, Christopher, 35 *Colours of Hope* (Kelling C.P. School)

Gee, Aileen, 120, 216 *Pen Flowers* (Wensum Lodge)

George, Aran, 174 *Colours of Hope* (Kelling C.P. School)

Gibran, Kahlil, 131 *The Prophet*

Glease, Angela, 168 *Something to Say* (Sheffield Diocesan Education Cttee)

Goodbourn, David, 204

Gor'ky, Maksim, 81

Grenfell, Joyce, 42 (Richard Scott Simon Ltd)

Ha'Elyon, Tami, 2 *My Shalom, My Peace* (Sabra Books)

Hamilton, Elizabeth, 115*

Harding, David J. 20, 227

Hares, G. Betty, 13 (first published in *Now)*

Harriott Fr John, 218 *Christian Aid News*

Hawkes, Susan, 181 (St Martin's Church, Knowle)

Head, Alison, 176 (first published in *Partners in Learning)*

Herbert, George, 138*

Herrick, Robert, 66*

Hewett, Anita, 61 *Something to Think About* (BBC Publications)

Hilton, Donald, 11, 27, 55, 57, 60, 113, 200

Hogben, Liz, 193

Hood, Thomas, 202*

Hopkins, Gerard Manley, 122*

Houselander, Caryll, 1, 3, 7 *The Flowering Tree* (Sheed & Ward Ltd)

Housman, Laurence, 12 *The Little Plays of St Francis* (Sidgwick & Jackson Ltd)

Julian, Lady, 63, 82, 161, 162 *Enfolded in Love* by Llewellyn (Darton, Longman & Todd Ltd)

Keller, Helen, 144

Kierkegaard, Søren, 141*

Kifle, Melaki, 201

Kilvert, Francis, 112, 203 *Kilvert's Diary* Ed William Plomer, by permission Sheila Hooper (Jonathan Cape Ltd)

Lawrence, D. H. 32, 74, 89, 105, 142*

Lee, R. S., 128, 163 *Your Growing Child and Religion* (Macmillan & Co Inc)

Lewis, A. J., 102 (first published in *Reform)*

Lewis, Joanna, 186 *Something to Say* (Sheffield Diocesan Education Cttee)

Lindsay, Elizabeth, 175, 195

Livingstone, David, 91*

Love, Martyn, 182 (Horfield C.E. School)

Lovestone, Laura, 194 (Archbishop Tenison's School)

Lubulwa, Godfrey, 231

Luthuli, Chief Albert, 208

McCormack, Phyllis, 192

McKay, Dermot, 14, 40 (Blandford Press Ltd)

Macdonald, George, 119★
Magdalene, Sister Sarah, 97 *More Wantage Poems* (A. R. Mowbray & Co Ltd)
Magee, J. G., 169 *The Teacher's World*
Mandala, Nelson, 207
Marais, Elizabeth, 189, 190
Marais, Michael, 30
Martyn, M. J., 123
Mattocks, Brewer, 152★
Meynell, Alice, 51★
Micklem, Caryl, 19
Millay, Edna St Vincent, 16 *Collected Poems* (Harper & Row) © 1928, 1955 by Edna St Vincent Millay and Norma Millay Ellis
Miller, Doris, 31
Milton, Gary, 180 (Horfield C.E. School)
Milton, Samantha, 96 *Something to Say* (Sheffield Diocesan Education Cttee)
Morely, Rebecca, 96 *Something to Say* (Sheffield Diocesan Education Cttee)
Moshe, Shai Ben, 220 *My Shalom, My Peace* (Sabra Books)
Mozart, W. A., 41 *The Many Faces of Grief* by Edgar N. Jackson (SCM Press Ltd)
Nehru Jawaharlal, 79 *The Fall of the British Empire* by Colin Cross (A. D. Peters & Co Ltd)
Newman, Cardinal, 83★
Nightingale, Florence, 196★
Oman, John, 92
Oosterhuis, Huub, 150 *Prayers, Poems and Songs* (Sheed & Ward Ltd)
Origen, 107★
Patey, Edward, 70 *Christian Life Style* (E. P. Publishing Ltd, a Division of A. & C. Black, Publishers, Ltd)
Peguy, Charles, 125★
Peter the Hermit, 58★
Phillips, J. B., 72 *Ring of Truth* (Hodder & Stoughton Ltd)
Pickard, Jan, 24 (first published in *Partners in Learning*)
Poore, Helen, 103 *Colours of Hope* (Kelling C.P. School)
Pope, Alexander, 170★
Press, John, 18
Raikes, Robert, 59★
Rambridge, Kate, 50 *Colours of Hope* (Kelling C.P. School)
Richards, Clare, 100
Riley, Julie, 179 (Horfield C.E. School)
Robinson, John, 133★
Rollison, Ian, 49 *Colours of Hope* (Kelling C.P. School)
Romero, Archbishop, 229
Roosevelt, Theodore, 88★
Rufeisen, Shalom, 224 *My Shalom, My Peace* (Sabra Books)
Salter, David, 185 *An Anthology of Poems* (Hethersett V.C. School)

Schweitzer, Albert, 69 *The Quest for the Historical Jesus*
Seattle, Chief, 37★
Shurek, Tali, 222 *My Shalom, My Peace* (Sabra Books)
Siang, Francis Khoo Kah, 210 (quoted in *Now*)
Slade, Donna, 172 *Something to Say* Sheffield Diocesan Education Cttee)
Solzhenitsyn, Alexander, 38, 86, 134, 148 *One Day in the Life of Ivan Denisovitch* (Victor Gollancz Ltd)
Southwell, Robert, 10★
Strong, William, 39
Studdert Kennedy, G. A., 54, 64, 75, 217★
Tagore, Rabindranath, 136 *Sadhana* (Macmillan Publishers Ltd)
Target, George, 184 *Pen Flowers* (Wensum Lodge)
Taylor, Cecily, 76 (first published in *Reform*)
Temple, William, 84, 118
Thai-Binh, Ngyuen, 6
Turner, P. W., 93, 106, 171 *Christ in the Concrete City*
Turner, Steve, 71, 109 © 1976 *Up to Date* (Hodder & Stoughton Ltd)
Uludong, Moses Y., 205 *Youth* (World Council of Churches)
Watson, Maureen, 198 *CCA News* (Christian Conference of Asia)
West, A. F., 46
Willey, Basil, 110 *Spots of Time* (The author's literary estate and Chatto & Windus)
Williams, H. A., 108 *True Resurrection*, 164 *The True Wilderness*
Wojtyla, Karol, 228 *Easter Vigil* (Hutchinson)
Wordsworth, William, 114★
Yeats, W. B., 116 *The Winding Stairs* (A. P. Watt Ltd)
Yevtushenko, Yevgeny, 215
Yosef, Matti, 223 *My Shalom, My Peace* (Sabra Books)
Yungblut, John, 80, 99 *The Teilhard Review*

Also reproduced by permission:
17, 127, 151 *Child in the Church* (British Council of Churches)
126 *Learning for Life* (ILEA)
167 (Women's World Day of Prayer)
5 *Morning, Noon and Night* (Church Missionary Society)
156 *Christian Aid News*
165 *Communion through Preaching* (Charles Scribner's Sons)

★non-copyright or out of copyright

INDEX OF FIRST LINES

A day is like a journey	60	His twilight years have merged	189
A fire-mist and a planet	160	How can I reach	190
A mother's caring	82	How do I know that God is good	54
Almighty God	166	I am dumb	231
Alone, alone	185	I am open to you, Lord	85
And a woman who held a babe	131	I asked God for strength	90
And he showed me more	63	I asked him once	81
And joy is everywhere	136	I believe in a colour blind God	155
As for what you call	125	I believe in God the Father	156
As in hoary winter's night	10	I believe in one world	153
As soon as he arrived in Taizé	226	I believe that there's	154
As truly as God is our father	161	I believe that nothing	45
As we live, we are transmitters	89	I cannot influence the fate	228
At last on the little black tree	3	I don't like wars	223
Autumn has gone	120	I had a paint-box	222
Because you are weak	129	I have longed	95
Be honest about violence	227	I have not have the leisure	59
Behind this door there sits	230	I have walked with people	144
Black is my mother's loving arms	198	I like to play	180
Blow coldly bitter over me	31	I live in a family	181
Brainwashing and indoctrination	126	I met a stranger yestere'en	68
But now you put a question to me	159	I never invited you	205
By rhythm we measure life	F	I remember, I remember	202
Christian nurture	151	I saw that God rejoices	162
Christ is risen indeed	106	I was hungry	213
Christ is the Lord of all	111	I would have given the church	196
Christmas is really	109	If a child lives with criticism	130
Christ on the cross	100	If, as a result of some	157
Clean your teeth!	179	If at any time they stop the	229
Come, Lord	5	If chance can dance	173
Conceived out of wedlock	13	If I should go	42
Creator God, with your feet	167	If Jesus was born today	73
Death is nothing at all	44	If patriotism be a virtue	225
Does the word 'Easter' occur	104	If you believe that Christ	107
Don't wait for an angel	19	If you can keep your head	191
Drinking drop by drop	6	If you leave me	43
During my lifetime	207	In '41 Mama took me	215
During the two years	117	In the early years of life	128
Each person is unique	188	In the light of evolution	99
Far in the distance	86	In the light of the incarnation	17
First it comes as a baby's hand	67	Is it possible	101
For, as far back as I can	132	Is it true that missionaries	91
For my part I cannot	133	Is this a Fast, to keep	66
For thine is the kingdom	74	It is not the critic who counts	88
For this your mother	16	It matters little where	37
For those who grasp	206	It ought to be lovely to be old	32
From the Christian point of view	21	It's dangerous to walk alone	140
Glistening, sparkling	34	It's easy to be happy	135
God did not send	15	I've made a home	178
God has created me	83	I've made the mistake	14
God made man to be free	139	Jesus is the normal child	127
Guardian of peace	103	Know then, thyself	170
He comes to us as one unknown	69	Let us open the clenched fist	218
He was like a powerful current	79	Like the gentle dew	25
Here are no signs of festival	18	Listen, I am the earth	62
Here beside the hedge I stand	123	Lord, thou knowest better	33
Here is a pair of hands	87	Love bade me welcome	138
Here is our cross	24	Male and female created he them	184

Methought that in a solemn	119
My fiftieth year	116
My gaze travels down	50
My heart leaps up	114
My house is large	177
Never forgotten	35
Nice and clinical	39
No frame	97
No happiness, no joy	36
No real cares	124
Nothing is so beautiful	122
Not ours, O Lord, but yours	200
Not Spring	27
O Lord, pardon me three sins	158
Oh hearken, for this is wonder	12
Oh I have slipped	169
Old people funny	197
Once, as I was looking	115
One day, when my sufferings	110
Peace is a young mother	220
Peace is like gossamer	219
Peace, we will get you	224
Perhaps the root	164
Poverty is the moment	214
Refugees are people	201
Safety is not behind	92
Screams, shouts, laughter	194
Shall I tell the Romans?	96
She is a reed	1
Short days of feeble sunlight	29
Shukhov went to sleep	134
Since death (properly understood)	41
So it's a bad winter	30
So tell me, what is joy	137
So you stepped out	53
Starting on the hill	46
Streaming through meadows	121
Sunday's the day for holy work	143
Thank God	20
That same evening	142
The band's a recommended way	149
The blood-red petals fall	216
The church—every gathering	147
The churches loudly assert	105
The circle of a girl's arms	7
The furious fantasia	174
The Lord is my pace-maker	77
The Lord is my pace-setter	78
The parish priest	152
The plane is off its course	40
The relevance of the father	163
The shadow of his later cross	11
The sin of Pilate	93
The towering peaks	49
The waiting is the best of it	22
The world is passing	58
The world's at winter's dusk	28
Then I saw the earth	176
There are not two separate	80
There are people after Jesus	71
There in the queue	148
There is a freedom	211
There is a sin	171
There is a world of wonder	64
These are the greedy days	4
This afternoon I walked	112
This is the church of my dreams	146
Thou art the way	51
Time to me is the plants	48
Today I will teach you roses	65
Travelling	52
Twinkle, twinkle	212
Walking on water	76
Waste of Muscle	217
We are all one	56
We built you a city	221
We dare to laugh in church	145
We seek the unity	55
We, the Peoples	209
We were busy all day	203
'Well,' he said conclusively	38
Well, that's a washout	23
What do we see, you ask	193
What do you see nurses	192
What happened to me	72
What is meant when we say	70
What is the sun	175
What is the use of words?	98
What is this place	150
What makes a person?	187
What shall I do today	168
When Adam delved	183
When my Dad	182
When my mam married Ray	186
When Peace will come	2
When the commandment	141
When the spent soil of summer	199
When through the whirl	75
When we begin to recognise	108
When winter is around us	113
While we deliberate, God reigns	118
While you're walking along	61
Who should we thank for plants	172
Who will deny that thirty years	208
William Beebee, the naturalist	165
Winter's coming	210
Winter creeps	26
Without listening	102
Worship is the submission	84
Yet if his Majesty	8
You bore him, fed him	9
You, in this New Year	47
You passed a resolution	204
You sow your seeds in spring	195
You told us	94
You worm!	57

SUBJECT INDEX

Reference is to item numbers. Numbers in *italics* indicate a whole Section.

abortion 39
accountability 132, 200
achievement 88
acorn 123
Adam 80, 183
adolescence 126, 129
Advent *1-6*, 8, 22, 25
adventure 53, 54, 88, 146, 169
aeroplane 40, 169
Africa 18, 91, 207
animals 61, 74, 122, 168, 181, 182
anonymity 8
anticipation 2-6, 81, 221, 223
apartheid 208, 211
armaments 2, 216, 224, 228
authority 132, 148
Autumn 27, 105, 120, *199-231*
baby 10, 39, 128, 131
Baptists 86
beauty 50, 64, 65, 124, 167, 176
Beebee, William 165
Beethoven 110
beginning 45
bereavement 42-44, 189
Bethlehem 11, 19, 24
Bible 133, 153, 205
birds 26, 57, 74, 120, 122, 123, 160,
  168, 176
birth 27, 128
blindness 144
brainwashing 126, 127, 151
bread 15, 150, 214, 215
brotherhood 37, 153, 155
brothers 181
Bunyan, John 110
Calvary 11, 24, 101, 160
challenge 146
chance 173
childhood 17, 124-128, 130, 131,
  163, 182, 186, 202
children 24, 59, 81, 109, 130-132,
  176, 179, 180, 182, 194
Christ:
  anonymity 68, 69, 71
  his birth 2, 4, 7-15, 17, 19, 25, 73,
    105
  his childhood 127
  his death 11, 16, 96, 97, 100-103,
    105, 147, 160
  his humanity 71, 72, 127, 155
  his lordship 74, 77, 111
  his message 156

Christ (continued):
  his ministry 70, 76, 78, 94-96, 98,
    99, 155
  his nature 78, 80, 82
  his rejection 8, 10, 11, 16, 19
  his resurrection 6, 8, 69, 102, 103,
    105-107, 111, 119
  his second coming 73, 75
  redeemer 25
Christmas 4, *7-25*, 109
Church 16, 52, 87, 119, 133, 143,
  145-147, 150, 152, 156, 196, 203,
  229
Church unity 55, 56
city 3, 106, 111, 176
colonialiam 37, 205
colours 168, 222
communication 16, 152, 231
confidence 128, 166
conscience 218
consecration 160
conservation 200
conversion 117
creation 48, 57, 61-65, 112, 115,
  123, 124, 136, 160, 165, 168, 172,
  174, 175, 199, 200
creativity 168
creeds 83, 153-157
cross 100, 101
darkness 12
dawn 113
day 60, 112
death 5, 27, 36, 39, 40-44, 52, 101,
  102, 149
destiny 37
disappointment 221
discipleship 19, 69, 83, 85, 87, 89,
  90, 92, 94, 119
discipline 87, 160, 196
disillusionment 23
diversity 55, 177
duty 160
earth 61, 62, 195, 199, 200
earthworm 57, 61
Easter 102, *104-119*
Eden 122, 184
education 59, 126
equality 156, 218, 225
Eve 97, 183
evolution 64, 80, 99, 160
exile 38
experience 125

exploration 49, 53, 91, 92, 126
faith 53, 54, 102, 139, 157
fame 40
family 179-182, 186
fast 4, 66
fatherhood 131, 161, 163, 180
fear 103, 110, 211
feast 4, 66
flowers 26, 50, 64, 65, 115, 120,
   121, 160, 168, 172, 173, 195, 199,
   203, 223, 224
freedom 38, 53, 103, 110, 124, 137,
   139, 156, 176, 188, 207, 209, 211
free will 184
friendship 33, 35, 36, 67
fulfilment 32, 44, 72
Galilee 106
Gandhi 79
generation gap 58, 129, 132, 179,
   180, 182
giving 89
God:
   and his Kingdom 56, 74, 97, 118
   creator 56, 156, 167, 168, 174
   his character 128, 159, 161-164,
     171
   his goodness 54
   his love 63
   his presence 52, 60, 113, 115, 152,
     158, 166, 169, 202
   his purpose 63
   word of 117, 133, 143, 150, 152
Good Friday 102, 105
Good News 4, 21, 24, 231
greed 4
grief 36, 43
growth 27, 62, 123, 126, 151, 163,
   182, 192
handicap 189-191, 194
hands 67
happiness 50, 86, 116, 117, 134,
   135, 211
harvest 203
hatred 12
hazelnut 63
hearing 65, 190
Holy Communion 95, 96, 145
Holy Spirit 171
home 38, 162, 177-179, 181
honesty 33
hope 2-4, 6, 47, 53, 102, 139, 154,
   214, 223, 224
hospital 192, 193
human nature 80, 140, 156, 162,
   170, 187-189, 192, 215, 230

human rights 155, 156, 183, 196,
   201, 204-206, 208, 209, 218, 225
humility 9, 11, 33, 40, 165, 171
hunger 204, 213
identity 13, 187-189, 191, 192, 201,
   215
idolatry 164, 171
imitation 130, 131
incarnation 15-18, 25, 64, 67, 68,
   72, 73, 75, 79, 152
indoctrination 126, 151
industry 75, 228
innocence 125, 202
insects 172
Joseph 24
journey 60
joy 15, 112, 116, 117, 122, 136, 137,
   143, 162, 176, 180
Judas 95, 96
justice 153, 155, 201, 209
kindness 40
laughter 145, 176
Lent *66-103*
Leonov, Alexei 53
light 12, 25, 106
loneliness 22, 23, 140, 178, 185, 186
longing 160
love 7, 12, 30, 39, 64, 94, 100, 102,
   117, 128, 129, 138, 139, 141, 142,
   176, 194, 219
marriage 111, 183, 184, 186
Martha 87
Mary 1, 7, 9, 11, 24
maturity 127
memory 35, 147, 197, 202, 210
Messiah 2
minerals 61, 200
mission 91, 143, 152, 205, 229, 231
mist 46
moderation 208
motherhood 128, 131, 160, 161, 220
Moscow 215
Mozart 41
music 110, 149
Nazareth 1, 99
new life 3
New Year *45-65*
night 5, 60, 113
nurture 126, 127, 131, 132, 151, 163
oak tree 31, 123
obedience 7, 9, 14, 69, 70, 83, 132
old age 31-33, 58, 114, 146, 167,
   176, 192, 193, 195
one world 153, 156, 204, 206-209,
   211, 225

openness 85
oppression 6, 201, 205-208, 229
parents 131, 132, 179-182, 186
partnership 183
Passover 95, 96
patience 33
patriotism 225
Paul, apostle 38
peace 1, 12, 50, 139, 176, 209, 218-225
Pentecost *133-171*
Pilate 93, 147
pilgrimage 46, 49-53, 55, 92
politics 109
potential 80, 230
poverty 6, 14, 24, 96, 204, 213, 214
power 148
prayer 38, 90
prison(ers) 21, 25, 38, 86, 134, 148, 149, 176, 206, 215
progress 81
prophet 229
purpose 14, 37, 40-42, 45, 50-52, 54, 60, 72, 81, 83, 88, 117, 154
racialism 14, 155, 156, 176, 207
rainbow 114
reconciliation 115
refugees 201, 204, 210, 226
Remembrance Sunday 216
responsibility 160
resurrection 3, 6, 102, 106-108, 110, 112, 114-116, 119, 155, 199
revolution 153
risk 53, 88
Romans 96
Roosevelt 165
rose 64, 65
Sacrament 82, 95, 96, 147, 150
sacrifice 91, 216
sadness 36
salvation 10
school 60
Schutz, Roger 236
seasons 27, 60, 104, 105, 109, 113, 120, 210
senses 65, 67, 144, 190
service 83, 87, 91, 94, 119, 143
shepherds 19, 24, 109
sight 65, 144

sin 93, 95, 100, 107, 110, 129, 138, 156, 158, 171, 184, 228
sisters 181
smell 65
snow 28, 30, 31, 120, 171
Socrates 160
space & exploration 53, 111, 165, 169, 212, 213
sparrow 30
Spirit of God 1
Spring 3, 26, 27, 30, 104, 109, 112, *120-132*, 195, 223
stars 11, 165
Summer 27, 105, *172-198*, 210
sun 46, 172, 174, 175, 202
Sunday 52, 86, 143, 145, 148
Sunday school 59, 196
survival 30
taste 65
Taizé 226
tears 34, 36, 64, 146, 190
tension 58
thankfulness 6, 20, 41, 135, 162, 172
time 48, 51
tolerance 209
touch 65, 67
tradition 6, 18, 147, 151
Trinity 161
trust 90, 128
United Nations 209
unity 56, 57, 64, 136, 139, 156, 176, 207, 220, 228
vegetable 195
violence 93, 226, 227
vulnerability 94, 219
war 2, 12, 209, 211, 212, 215-217, 220, 222-225, 227, 228
waste 217
water 6, 57, 62, 76, 172, 176
wind 31
Winter *26-44*, 113, 120, 176, 210
wonder 64, 112, 114, 115, 123
Word of God 1, 133, 143, 150, 152
work 75, 81, 89, 119
worship 84, 86, 95, 146, 150, 171, 203, 226
youth 58, 126, 129, 146, 167, 217